Reminiscence reviewed

RETHINKING AGEING SERIES

Series editor: Brian Gearing
Department of Health and Social Welfare
The Open University

The rapid growth in ageing populations in Britain and other countries has led to a dramatic increase in academic and professional interest in the subject. Over the past decade this has led to the publication of many research studies which have stimulated new ideas and fresh approaches to understanding old age. At the same time, there has been concern about continued neglect of ageing and old age in the education and professional training of most workers in health and social services, and about inadequate dissemination of the new information and ideas about ageing to a wider public.

This series aims to fill a gap in the market for accessible, up-to-date studies of important issues in ageing. Each book will focus on a topic of current concern addressing two fundamental questions: what is known about this topic? And what are the policy, service and practice implications of our knowledge? Authors will be encouraged to develop their own ideas, drawing on case material, and their own research, professional or personal experience. The books will be interdisciplinary, and written in clear, non-technical language which will appeal to a broad range of students, academics and professionals with a common interest in ageing and age care.

Current and forthcoming titles:
Simon Biggs and Chris Phillipson: **Elder abuse in perspective**
Ken Blakemore and Margaret Boneham: **Age, race and ethnicity:**
    A comparative approach
Joanna Bornat (ed.): **Reminiscence reviewed: Evaluations,**
    achievements, perspectives
Bill Bytheway: **Ageism**
Julia Johnson: **Structured dependency and older people**
Moira Sidell: **Health in later life: Unravelling the mystery**
Christina Victor: **Rethinking community care for older people**

Reminiscence reviewed
Evaluations, achievements, perspectives

EDITED BY
JOANNA BORNAT

OPEN UNIVERSITY PRESS
Buckingham · Philadelphia

Open University Press
Celtic Court
22 Ballmoor
Buckingham
MK18 1XW

and
1900 Frost Road, Suite 101
Bristol, PA 19007, USA

First Published 1994

A catalogue record of this book is available from the British Library

ISBN 0 335 19041 3 (pb) 0 335 19042 1 (hb)

Library of Congress Cataloging-in-Publication Data

Reminiscence reviewed: evaluations, achievements, perspectives/
    edited by Joanna Bornat
        p.   cm. – (Rethinking ageing)
    Includes bibliographical references and index.
    ISBN 0 335 19042 1   ISBN 0 335 19041 3 (pbk.)
    1. Gerontology – Biographical methods.   I. Bornat, Joanna
II. Series
HQ1061.R43   1993
305.26'0723 – dc20   93–22968
                                                                     CIP

Typeset by Type Study, Scarborough
Printed in Great Britain by Biddles Limited, Guildford and Kings Lynn

Contents

Notes on contributors

JOHN ADAMS is a Nurse Teacher at the Sir Gordon Roberts College of Nursing and Midwifery, Kettering General Hospital, Northamptonshire. He has a special interest in reminiscence activities in the institutional setting.

DOROTHY ATKINSON is a Senior Lecturer in the School of Health, Welfare and Community Education. Her background is in social work and social work education, and includes several years' experience of working with people with learning difficulties. Her Open University work has been primarily in the learning disability field.

DR MIKE BENDER, a Clinical Psychologist, worked for many years in a social services department in the East End of London, leading a team of psychologists who provided services to all the major client groups. For his work in applying psychology in community settings, he was made a Fellow of the British Psychological Society in 1981. Since 1988, he has been Head of Psychological Services to Older People in Plymouth Health Authority. The author of some fifty articles and three books, he wrote *Groupwork with the Elderly* with Andrew Norris and Paulette Bauckham, and his major interest is the uses of therapeutic groupwork.

JOANNA BORNAT is a Lecturer in the School of Health, Welfare and Community Education at the Open University where she has worked on courses on ageing and community care. She has a longstanding interest and involvement in reminiscence work with older people and in oral history. She is joint editor of the journal *Oral History*.

KEVIN BUCHANAN is a Lecturer in Social Psychology in the Faculty of Humanities and Social Science, Nene College, Moulton Park, Northampton. He is currently engaged in doctoral research applying discourse analysis to reminiscence work.

PETER COLEMAN is Professor in Social Gerontology at the University of Southampton, a joint appointment between Geriatric Medicine and Social Work Studies. His research interests are in the study of identity processes, biography and meaning in later life.

PATRICIA DUFFIN has worked with older people in hospital and sheltered housing. She has trained health, social services and adult education staff working with older people. She has published in the fields of adult basic education and reminiscence. She is co-founder of Gatehouse Publishing Charity Ltd, Manchester.

JEFFREY GARLAND, a Clinical Psychologist for 28 years (and still learning), is Consultant with the Department of Psychiatry of Old Age, Mental Health Unit, Oxfordshire District Health Authority.

FAITH GIBSON is a Reader in Social Work at the University of Ulster. She has studied humanities, social work and education in the Universities of Sydney, Queensland and Chicago and practised as a social worker in child care, mental health and services for older people.

JOHN HARRIS, of the Department of Applied Social Studies at the University of Warwick, has worked as a social worker, training officer and manager in a social services department. In those posts, he had a special interest in work with older people. His publications include *Management Skills in Social Care*, with Des Kelly (Gower, 1991).

TOM HOPKINS' interest in reminiscence began while teaching social work to students working with older people in residential and day-care settings. He is now an independent consultant and trainer in social work and higher education.

ROSIE MERE, since coming to the UK in 1989 from New Zealand via Australia, has been working as an arts trainer in hospitals, homes and day centres throughout Wales. She is currently working as a full-time mental health professional in Wales.

DAVID MIDDLETON is a Senior Lecturer in Psychology in the Department of Human Sciences and a member of the Discourse and Rhetoric Group at Loughborough University. A study of remembering as a form of social activity is his principal research interest.

PAM SCHWEITZER is the Artistic Director of Age Exchange Theatre Trust. She directs the company's professional theatre productions and edits their books of reminiscences. Pam has developed the first Reminiscence Centre in London for cultural, inter-generational and training activities related to reminiscence.

Series editor's preface

The rapid growth in ageing populations in this and other countries has led to a dramatic increase in academic and professional interest in gerontology. Since the mid-1970s, we have seen a steady growth in the publication of British research studies which have attempted to define and describe the characteristics and needs of older people. Equally significant have been the very few theoretical attempts to re-conceptualize what old age means and to explore new ways in which we think about older people (e.g. Johnson 1976; Townsend 1981; Walker 1981). These two broad approaches which can be found in the literature on ageing – the descriptive (what do we know about older people) and the theoretical (what do we understand about older people and what does old age mean to them) – can also be found in the small number of postgraduate and professional training courses in gerontology which are principally intended for those who work with older people in the health and social services.

Concurrent with this growth in research and knowledge, however, has been a growing concern about the neglect of ageing and old age in the education and basic training of most workers in the health and social services, and about inadequate dissemination of the new information and ideas about ageing to lay carers and a wider public. There is, therefore, a widening gap between what we now know and understand about ageing and ageing populations and the limited amount of knowledge and information which is readily available and accessible to the growing number of professional and voluntary workers and others who are involved in the care of older people.

The main aim of the 'Rethinking Ageing' series is to fill this gap with books which will focus on a topic of current concern or interest in ageing. These will include elder abuse, health and illness in later life, community care and working with older people. Each book will address two fundamental questions: What is known about this topic and what are the policy and practice implications of this knowledge?

Reminiscence Reviewed: Evaluations, Achievements, Perspectives is a highly appropriate topic with which to launch a series called 'Rethinking Ageing'. Attitudes towards reminiscence have undergone a fundamental reappraisal during the past 30 years. Joanna Bornat refers in her excellent historical Introduction to this volume to Robert Butler's influential paper, 'The life review: An interpretation of reminiscence in the aged' (1963), where he argued that, far from being something which should be discouraged in older people, or written off as mere nostalgia for the past, reminiscence was a natural and universal human process which could have positive outcomes as people face old age. In Britain, Malcolm Johnson's 1976 paper, 'That was your life: A biographical approach to later life', influenced gerontological thinking about the value of considering older people's past lives and their relevance to present needs. It also argued a persuasive case for 'biographical listening' in the hope that researchers and practitioners would pay attention to older people's own definitions of their needs. Johnson's argument struck a chord among those of us who had grown dissatisfied with the low priority accorded to social work with older people. A common assumption of the time was that older people's needs could be met automatically through a very limited, fixed range of services – usually a home help, delivered meal, or a place in a residential home. I remember vividly in 1974 a social work colleague, professionally trained in child care work, who boasted that he could assess an older person's need for a place in a residential home in a single ten-minute interview, a practice which, if similarly applied to children or young people, he would have rightly found appalling.

A decade or so later I contributed along with Malcolm Johnson, Tim Dant and Michael Carley to the Gloucester Care for Elderly People at Home research and development project (Dant *et al.* 1990). An innovative feature of the project was its attempt to find a practical application for the biographical approach through a biographically based interview method for assessing older people's health and social services' needs. By trying to understand their current needs in a context of their past experience, we hoped that there would be a consequent improvement in the appropriateness and acceptability of services offered.

A starting point for the research team were three convictions which we had gained from our previous experience of life history and biographical research and which seemed relevant to older people's needs in this context. These were: (1) by listening to life histories of older people a worker can gain a different and more fully rounded view of their personality and needs; (2) reminiscence can enhance self-esteem; (3) the way people cope with loss in later life is dependent on earlier life experiences and on valued present relationships and activities. Our research task was to develop an approach to assessment which reflected these principles and was also demonstrably effective and efficient when employed in the everyday practice of health care professionals. It had to work within that specific context in order to meet its aim of eliciting a view of the older person's needs which would also lead to more varied and satisfying forms of assistance.

The Gloucester research project did succeed in demonstrating the value of the biographical approach to assessment and meeting the needs of individuals (Boulton *et al.* 1987; Dant *et al.* 1990). However, our experience of that project suggested that if reminiscence and biographical understanding are to be systematically used as part of the repertoire of practice skills of health professionals, social workers and others, a sensitive balance has to be struck between the often time-consuming, discursive and client-directed process of biographical inquiry through interviews, and the operational imperatives of being problem-focused and economical with time and effort.

In thinking further about how this experience could be translated from an action-research project to the everyday practice of professionals, we came to a conclusion which is echoed by some of the contributors to this book, who also reflect on the experience of using reminiscence in practice. Namely, it has to be done through a means which enables the worker or carer to understand and feel comfortable with the *principles* of the biographical and life-history approach and to incorporate it into his or her own style of working. The successful application in the Gloucester project of an approach based on biography and reminiscence resulted more from this sensitive and flexible application of the *principles* of an approach to biographical assessment by our interviewers to the differing personalities and circumstances of their clients, than it did to any strict adherence to a pre-formulated set of methods and processes devised initially by the research team. From this we drew a wider conclusion of relevance to other kinds of reminiscence work: that the biographical approach to assessment is precisely that, an *approach* which can be learned and adapted and employed in the light of particular circumstances and constraints which differ from one professional–client/patient context to another, rather than a 'tool' which practitioners should be expected to apply in a fixed or uniform way.

A similarly flexible emphasis on the principles involved in reminiscence work with older people, rather than on a fixed method or technique, is to be found in many of the papers in this volume. In this and other ways, the book demonstrates the maturing of reminiscence work as it has developed in theory and reflective practice in a variety of settings during the last two decades. Like the Gloucester project research team, Joanna Bornat believes that a legacy of much work of this kind is an education and training programme for workers with older people. It is to be hoped that this book, with its timely and critical reassessment of the value of reminiscence work in different areas of practice, may make its own contribution to such a programme.

Brian Gearing

Introduction

_____ JOANNA BORNAT _____

We are as strangers from another planet. How much do sociologists and psychologists, who spend their time peering at us through microscopes, measuring our reactions and performance as though we were Skinner's rats — how can they possibly understand our past in a world now so remote? Their academic training and life style totally unfit them for an understanding of the lives a greater portion of these elderly have led. Experience is the only reality.

(Elder 1977:72)

Gladys Elder 'OAP' made her plea for a greater understanding of the lives and experience of older people in the mid-1970s. Those of us who, in the intervening years, turned to ways of working with older people which value experience by encouraging remembering and reminiscing were probably tempted to think that we had identified the response to the need she identifies. Indeed, the period which followed saw an enthusiastic, almost evangelistic commitment to 'reminiscence therapy' or 'reminiscence work'.

This book brings together the work of practitioners some of whom have been formative in this development from its earliest years, others who arrived later but whose experience is nonetheless significant. Each contributor has been invited to review his or her engagement with reminiscence. Each was asked to reflect self-critically and with the objective of pointing up dilemmas, insights and pointers for future work. In this introduction, I set the scene with a brief historical account of the emergence of reminiscence work in Britain and then introduce the authors, showing the links, connections and common themes in their different accounts.

The Reminiscence Aids Project, funded by the then Department of Health and Social Security between 1978 and 1979, provided a launching pad for what I have described elsewhere as a 'social movement' (Bornat 1989). The project's early publicity for experiments with sounds and images among elderly residents and patients in homes and hospitals in the London area, drew immediate interest. Articles appeared in the professional press, a Sunday newspaper and, through Reuters, in the world's newspapers. Radio broadcasts brought letters from older people. One prolific correspondent joined the project's advisory team.

The long-term objectives of the Reminiscence Aids Project were to 'provide a framework for caring interactions', to 'restore a sense of personal value' and for older people 'to regain a fuller perspective of their own past lives, the better to relate to the present'. For the short term, the project aimed to produce 'an apparatus . . . using photographic slides and tape recorded sound, which will increase reminiscence in the elderly with mental infirmity' (DHSS 1979:4). This short-term objective was to be achieved in part after the project moved to Help the Aged Education Department following a change of government and the end of state funding. The images and sounds which had been collected and tested were transformed into six sequences of slides and tapes and published in 1981 as *Recall*. Demand for *Recall* packs far exceeded first expectations. As someone who was involved in the project once it moved to Help the Aged, I can recall our amazement at the response which came from all over the British Isles to what we had perceived as initially a model to be developed, complemented and improved to suit varying contexts and experiences (Help the Aged Education Department 1981:18).

Recall's importance lay in its apparent simplicity. A cassette player, slide projector and white wall were within the means of most institutions and community settings. Showing the sequences led to an instant response as people identified with the images, joined in with some of the music and songs or, sometimes, questioned what they saw. *Recall* played a part in popularizing reminiscence-based activities in the UK. By this stage, however, a shift in focus had already begun to develop. The Reminiscence Aids Project had originally set out to stimulate reminiscence among 'the elderly with mental infirmity'. Success in achieving this objective was evaluated when reactions among people in the early stages of dementia were tested during exposure to reminiscence. The findings were inconclusive, no effect on the ability to reminisce was observed (DHSS 1979:49). The result was that, in the early years at least, many organizers of reminiscence-based activities tended to exclude those seen as more 'difficult' or unmanageable. A purely medical model of their illness supported the maintenance of such boundaries (Kitwood and Bredin 1992).

Recall made a dramatic, if formulaic intervention, raising general awareness of reminiscence as an activity. More significant for the development of practice, including the sensitive understanding of reminiscence as a process, were the observations of psychologists, nurses, social care workers, gerontologists and other professionals whose work with older people focused around issues connected more with meeting basic needs: social, practical and emotional. Several contributors to this book point to Robert Butler's (1963) paper, 'The life review: An interpretation of reminiscence in the aged', as an inspiration, a form of legitimation at a time when reminiscing was seen as an unhealthy activity for older people (Dobrof 1984a:xvii–xv). Butler's argument was that life review is a natural and universal human mental process which may be positively helpful in dealing with those existential issues which accompany ageing. Life review as a form of helpful intervention was taken up by psychologists including Andrew Norris, Mike Bender, Peter Coleman and Jeffrey Garland. Under their influence, reminiscence came to be a guided and structured form of self-exploration, a means to explaining and reviewing a life, through personal accounting. Their aim, as clinical psychologists, was to find helpful ways for older people to resolve painfully lasting dilemmas. Working with individuals and with groups, their work was – and remains – therapeutic in intent.

Developing alongside this practice has been an awareness of the contribution which a biographical approach can make to meeting need in old age. Malcolm Johnson (1976) argued for an approach to the assessment of need which listened to accounts drawn from individual life-histories. He argued that the traditional approach to measurement of need, matched to a fixed range of services, such as home helps or meals on wheels, neglected the whole person. He suggested an approach to assessment which incorporated details of a life-history as a means to understanding present needs and wishes. This more instrumental (Bornat and Adams 1992) approach to reminiscence has been followed up in a number of different settings. Such diverse areas of provision as meals on wheels (Johnson *et al.* 1980), sheltered housing (Fielden, 1990), community care (Boulton *et al.* 1987), continuing care (Evers, 1981; Adams 1986) and residential care (Baines *et al.* 1987; Hockey 1989) have seen the development of approaches in which the eliciting of life-histories contributes to the negotiation of care plans and more sensitive and appropriate meeting of need. The same focus has been used in work with children and young people preparing for adoption (Ryan and Walker 1985) and with people with learning difficulties preparing to leave long-stay institutions (Fido and Potts 1989). This instrumental approach is distinctive for its assumption that the social worker, community worker, nurse or informal carer plays a part in the process of prompting reminiscence as part of his or her repertoire of skills.

Therapeutic and instrumental approaches to reminiscence work with older people have been accompanied by approaches which focus on development and learning outcomes. Adult educationalists and community education workers stress the importance of the process of working with memories of the past with a view to arriving at a product: an exhibition, book, sound tape or video (Duffin 1992; Lawrence and Mace 1992). Sharing the product with younger people, family members and the wider community means strengthening and building ties, an enhanced sense of worth and a perspective of change and development for the oldest and most frail person.

Closely associated with these developments was the work of oral historians (Samuel 1975; Thompson 1988; White 1980) and of practitioners with an interest in oral history (Adams 1984; Wright 1986). Oral history values memory as a source of information about the past. The boundary between reminiscence work and oral history is finely drawn but forms around a focus on content, rather than process. Groups of older people, with or without group facilitators whose main concern is the retrieval of past experience and its recording or preservation, in some way can be said to be taking part in oral history. When those same groups share memories with a view to understanding each other, or a shared situation, or with the aim of bringing about some change in their current lives, they are involved in reminiscence work.

Similarly, the interviewer who focuses on a life-history with a view to learning about the past and an individual's part in that past, is working as an oral historian. The interviewer who encourages life-review covering those same events and experiences but with a view to promoting greater self-awareness and personal reflection by the older person, is engaging in reminiscence. The difference is fine and indeed the most rewarding experiences occur when there is awareness and promotion of links between the two perspectives (Adams 1984; Bornat 1989; Grele 1991).

As interest and involvement in reminiscence work grew, an identifiable 'school' emerged, with leaders and proselytizers who found a ready audience among staff working with older people in residential homes, hospitals and day-care facilities. Taking part in reminiscence groups we felt, like Studs Terkel, who describes his emotion on meeting Bertrand Russell and shaking the hand of the man who shook the hand of the man who shook the hand of Napoleon (Terkel 1986:64), that we were literally talking to the past. Older people taking part gained recognition of past selves, interests and achievements, a form of immortality gained through passing on accounts of individual lives. In groups and in individual exchanges, we heard not only public accounts but also individual, minority experiences and participated in giving recognition and worth to forgotten or suppressed accounts (Lai *et al.* 1986). We were taking part in a learning process which drew in carers, staff and a wide range of age groups. We met nursing and care staff who saw the potential of this approach for their own personal and professional development and who found ways of incorporating past lives into assessment procedures and care plans, challenging the worst aspects of institutional life and their own often undervalued status (Woods *et al.* 1992). Finally, we felt that we were involved in a form of subversion through the celebration of ordinary life-experiences and by providing alternatives to a history which was more usually the story of the lives of the rich and powerful in society (Thompson 1978). And our partners in subversion were older people whose individual and diverse identities and whose status had been threatened and undermined by western society's particular ways of dealing with becoming older (Elder 1977; Phillipson 1982). There were latent values threading through this developing practice, a commitment to self-determination, empowerment, individuality and social integration.

But there were cautionary accounts and critiques. Several of the authors in this book refer to limited experimental evidence, surveys of work in the field and more guarded estimates of the outcomes of reminiscence work. Over the years, there has been criticism of the content of some reminiscence programmes, the slide into routinized entertainment, the tendency to celebrate the past rather than to acknowledge real pain and difficult emotions engendered by remembering (Thornton and Brotchie 1987; Bornat 1989). There has also been a growing recognition that skills in communication, understanding, resourcing and goal-setting required the collaboration and consent of the older people involved, as well as the cooperation of colleagues, managers and co-professionals (Gibson 1989a).

Evaluation of reminiscence has tended to be restricted to experimentally designed interventions and studies. Such projects, mainly US based, have relied on the formal measurement of defined characteristics such as mood, behaviour traits, anxiety, self-worth, cognitive levels and depression. Few included people with dementing illness. Almost all involve relatively short periods of observation under controlled conditions (Haight 1991). More rare have been studies such as Peter Coleman's (1986), which relied on observation and evaluation of people's use of reminiscence over a longer period of time.

All the authors in this book were invited to reflect on their experience as people who have engaged in reminiscence work. Controlled experiments have their place in the development of tested concepts and theories. However, the importance of reflection on the part of practitioners is now increasingly valued as a source of critical awareness and a means to learning (Schon 1990). All the writers were invited to reflect critically on their own experience as facilitators of reminiscence and to draw out conclusions from this process of self-evaluation.

The book falls into two parts. The first six chapters each take a discursive view of reminiscence work from the writer's own experience or of practice observed. Then, Chapters 7–11 each draw on experience of work within a specific setting or with a particular group of people. Peter Coleman reflects on the idea of life-history work as story-telling and argues for a perspective which attributes continuing roles and relevance for older people in late twentieth-century western society. His focus on reminiscence as 'self-preservation' guides us towards a recognition that reminiscence has a range of different functions.

Jeffrey Garland, writing from the perspective of the clinical psychologist, reviews the literature of life-review therapy and finds a role for reminiscence. He describes opportunities for clients to gain greater control not only in terms of their own self-knowledge but also in relation to the therapist. Although he argues that life-review may be 'a component of many therapeutic approaches' (p. 31), he is also clear that for some people there may be negative outcomes.

Mike Bender reviews his experience of working with groups of people, some living in residential care, others moving back into the community from long-term institutional care. Though he argues against the idea of reminiscence as therapy, he sees reminiscence groups as therapeutic and insists on a perspective which involves a sense of purpose for participants. Faith Gibson draws on examples of work with people with dementing illness in order to test the limits of reminiscence work. Her experience leads her to suggest a role for reminiscence in helping carers to respond to anxieties and to develop sympathetic and supportive care plans. The importance of understanding reminiscence as a social phenomenon is stressed in Kevin Buchanan and David Middleton's use of discourse analysis. They suggest dilemmas between what is claimed for reminiscence-based interventions and what is possible in practice. John Harris and Tom Hopkins argue the case for an approach to reminiscence work that is non-discriminatory. Reviewing the way in which reminiscence project work has taken its place in social work training, they take a critical look at reminiscence work which focuses exclusively on age while ignoring the key social divisions of class and race.

The five chapters which follow each review reminiscence work in a particular context. John Adams looks back, in the light of recent approaches towards a taxonomy of reminiscence, to interviews with his patients on a continuing care ward which he conducted some years earlier. He finds new understanding in the accounts presented to him by women who were becoming increasingly frail and facing death. Dorothy Atkinson's account of developing a book of memories with a group of older people with learning difficulties illustrates the role of reminiscence in reconstructing the past when a long institutional life has seemed to obliterate individuality. Pam Schweitzer describes the development of her work with reminiscence as drama, illustrating the process involved in transforming individual accounts into shared performance. Patricia Duffin is an adult educationalist who works on literacy programmes. Her approach means that she places a high value on the written text. She describes how she came to a compromise over this goal as she worked with patients on a continuing care ward and with tenants in a sheltered housing unit. Finally, Rosie Mere describes how she takes the theme of life story-telling in her work with people with mental health problems.

The chapters divide into two parts, but the accounts may be read in ways which draw themes from these different evaluations and perspectives. The idea of the narrative, the telling of a story as therapeutic and restorative in later life, indeed at the end of life, is a theme which dominates the contributions from Peter Coleman, Rosie Mere, Pam Schweitzer and John Adams. The critical role of the facilitator and the need for awareness of objectives is stressed by Dorothy Atkinson, Mike Bender, Faith Gibson, John Harris and Tom Hopkins, and Rosie Mere. Each of these authors generates their own guidelines for sensitive and successful groupwork.

A reading which focuses on the processes of groupwork takes in Mike Bender, Patricia Duffin, Faith Gibson and Dorothy Atkinson's chapters. In contrast, the role of the individual working in a one-to-one relationship links contributions from Peter Coleman, Jeffrey Garland and John Adams. The perspective of the care worker and the appropriation of reminiscence as an aspect of care delivery, is evaluated in chapters by Faith Gibson, Mike Bender, John Adams, Pam Schweitzer and John Harris and Tom Hopkins. Finally, a critical appreciation of the need to identify the social context and structural constraints surrounding reminiscence work is addressed in the chapters by John Harris and Tom Hopkins, and by Kevin Buchanan and David Middleton.

As well as links, there are opportunities for comparison among the chapters. For example, we find different accounts of research and evaluation. As Faith Gibson and Kevin Buchanan and David Middleton point out, reminiscence encompasses a wide range of diverse practice and understanding. Hence the need for variability in the forms of evaluation adopted. Differences in method are matched by differences in theorizing and conceptualizing the ageing process. Peter Coleman revisits disengagement theory, John Harris and Tom Hopkins' approach fits in with a political economy of old age, while Mike Bender and Jeffrey Garland in different ways take a focus which stresses compensation for loss of social role and identity. We also find examples of work with different groups. This reflects a diversity which initially the Reminiscence Aids Project and *Recall* scarcely acknowledged. However, this diversity is both linked and sustained by a commitment to a basic philosophy of individuality, empowerment, self-determination and social integration for all older people, irrespective of any disadvantage they may be experiencing.

From beginnings which promised much in terms of excitement and enjoyment, for older people and for carers and workers, ideas and approaches to reminiscence work have been much refined. The process has been one of self-criticism and reflection and, with the perspectives presented here, enables us to consider developing future work with perhaps greater sensitivity and more flexibility, but with no less confidence in our skills or goals.

What might these skills and goals be? Sensitive reminiscence work, as the chapters in this book testify, relies on an understanding both of debates in the literature and of careful evaluation of work in progress. Critiques of life-history and reminiscence work help to set limits and to develop awareness of what is both achievable and significant. The ability to review practice and to compare results across settings and including the views of participants should be an essential aspect of the work. Thus, for example, a recent article which takes a social constructionist perspective, suggesting that life-review is a social activity generated by the specific 'narrative challenges' of simply being old rather than by psychodevelopmental tasks (Wallace 1992), argues the need to review literature in the related fields of quality of life measures and of conversational analysis. It also suggests possibilities for reviewing practice in groupwork and within institutional settings.

Recent reviews of reality orientation (Woods 1992) and the development of validation therapy (Feil 1982) encourage a focus on normalization and valuing feelings expressed in working with people who have dementing illness. Sensitive and meaningful reminiscence work can include aspects of both approaches within a repertoire of skills. Knowledge of someone's past may help to decode behaviour in the present and a focus on valuing communication affirms that we are all, whatever our condition, social beings (Haight 1992).

In addition to skills in literature reviewing and in evaluation and reflection, sensitive and appropriately designed reminiscence work depends on its appropriation by the whole staff group into working and caring practices. The chapters in this book testify to the importance of securing the cooperation of all staff in the organization or unit in support of reminiscence work. This presupposes the need for awareness of the rewards of the approach to be a part of staff training at all levels. It also requires a commitment of resources in terms of staff time and budgets if such work is to be supported and not seen simply as a dispensable 'add on' or routinized activity. Incorporation into training for all staff members requires attention being given to groupwork skills, resourcing, communication and goal-setting.

Finally, if reminiscence work is to retain its position as empowering and enhancing, if Gladys Elder's prescription is to be attempted, then an essential component of the skill base for practitioners must be an awareness of advocacy and a valuing of diversity in the lives of older people. While reminiscence can clearly become a basis for self-advocacy for those with great mental frailty, as a process it must begin with consent and genuine participation. And, while reminiscence work enables the recognition of shared experience and helps to build collective ties, it must always sustain an ability to differentiate experience and to value that individuality which guarantees esteem and understanding in old age.

1

Reminiscence within the study of ageing: The social significance of story

—— PETER COLEMAN ——————————

Introduction: telling one's life-story

Reflection on the nature and purpose of reminiscence in later life takes one to the heart of social gerontology. Moreover, it touches many of the central issues in the study of the life-span as a whole. An interest in reminiscing links subjects as distinct as the psychology of memory and social anthropology. For it leads to an examination of the dynamic and creative forces that mould what is remembered and what is forgotten, as well as of older people's potential and actual role as tenders of culture and tradition. As they grow older and perspective on past and future changes, many people feel the need to explore and draw out meaning from their life-story, for the benefit of others as well as themselves, perhaps to seek reconciliation with its limitations and failings, and to achieve what Erik Erikson (1950) has called 'ego integrity'. Others reminisce for more pressing reasons as they try to hang on to a sense of who they are amidst life circumstances which have changed out of all recognition.

But a common element in all reminiscing is the possession of a life-story, an autobiography unique to each person. The importance of having a story to tell is evident early in life but becomes more urgent in middle age as the perceived end of life comes into view. The personal story is increasingly likely to be seen as a whole entity, one to be refined and elaborated on and in which to discern major themes. But not all of us succeed in producing an integrated account of our lives, or one with which we can live peacefully. For the character in Samuel Beckett's 'Krapp's Last Tape', the overwhelming impression is disgust. Probably more common than disgust is a feeling of void or haze. In modern western society, some people appear surprisingly blank about their lives, recalling only the most general outlines (Rabbitt 1988). This may be because they have never valued their experience of life or realized its value to others, and have therefore never learned to recount it.

For the life-story that is created not only has to make sense to the person but also has to be communicated to a wider audience if it has to have continued meaning. This I would suggest is one of the essential tasks of ageing, and one which we may at times need to help people to achieve, or even stand in their place to create for them if frailty has taken away their mental powers. Studies on our own geriatric wards in Southampton indicate that a substantial minority, perhaps as many as one-third, of very old people feel they would like to tell their life-story but do not have available listeners.

Allowing the person to have a voice and the opportunity for genuine self-expression are prerequisites for achieving a sense of control over life, and such control is vital if we are to take a consumer approach to services seriously. In fact there is a close connection between the telling of a life-story and examining the provisions we make for living in old age, as Malcolm Johnson and colleagues have stressed (Johnson 1976; Gearing and Dant 1990). Service providers need to ask themselves whether older people are able to relate their present circumstances to the life they have lived. It is important to note that this is not necessarily a question about the consistency of a person's life-story over time but of its coherence as a whole (Cohler 1982). Do the present circumstances fit, can they be made to fit in the story, or are they only worthless appendages?

I have tried so far to formulate a unifying theme for understanding the importance of reminiscence in terms of respecting and enabling the creation of the individual's life-story. But it also needs to be stressed how very varied the more immediate functions of reminiscence can be. There is a tendency on the part of some listeners to respond in a standard way to older people's reminiscences and to be insensitive to the particular purposes that lie behind any episode of returning to the past.

One way in which I have tried to reconcile this contrast between unity and diversity of purpose in reminiscence is to see the formulation of an ever more coherent life-story that demands to be told as an ultimate goal for every individual, whereas the obstacles along the way to its fulfilment are distinct for each person. Some may have literally forgotten what they have done, perhaps because they have never learned to value their achievements and experience. Others may not be able to see that a connection can be made between what they have achieved in the past and the challenges that face them now. There may be particular episodes in some people's lives which they have deliberately and successfully shut out of consciousness because they were unable to come to terms with them. Yet now they may feel the need to tell the whole story. Some, indeed, may feel overwhelmed by a sense of dissatisfaction and apply a theme of failure to their whole life-story.

A common approach to people's reminiscences is not feasible or appropriate. In recent years, a more differential approach has been neglected as workers have sought to establish the value of reminiscence as a worthwhile and enjoyable activity for older people, particularly in institutional settings. This enthusiasm has been understandable given the negative attitude to reminiscence that underlay thinking in work with elderly people up to the 1960s. In fact, to appreciate current attitudes to reminiscence and how they could be improved it is worth making a historical survey to see how we have arrived at our present position. Just as in getting to know an individual we can find out much about their present needs by working through their life-history with them, so we can learn much from examining the origin of ideas that currently excite or disturb us.

Early ideas on reminiscence

People have been pondering the significance of reminiscence in old age for a long time. Aristotle's statement is rightly well-known: 'they live by memory rather than by hope for what is left to them of life is but little compared to the long past' (Treatise on Rhetoric). This is an interesting comment because it links reminiscence with hope, another important theme in ageing (Lieberman and Tobin 1983). Aristotle opposes hope and reminiscence. Later we shall see that there are strong grounds for questioning this pessimistic attitude and claiming to the contrary that reminiscence can be an important constituent in safeguarding hope. Aristotle's melancholic view of older people's reminiscence accords with his very negative views on older people generally. He calls them irresolute, without positive opinions, pessimistic, small-minded and cowardly, and (in his Politics) concludes that they should be barred from political office because of their inflexibility and lack of moral feeling. Aristotle's views in fact reflect an element in classical Greek culture unsympathetic to ageing. This is perhaps related to the great value the Greeks gave to physical beauty: 'the gods too detest old age' says Aphrodite in Homer's *Iliad*.

Aristotle's attitude to ageing is of particular importance because of his influence on later western thinking, in particular the development of rational methods of enquiry, to which the rediscovery of his writings in the middle ages gave a considerable spur. One cannot help but wonder why he came to such negative conclusions on older people. It is likely that they were based on his own personal experience and observation of older people in the society around him.

Aristotle's views contrast strongly with the views of a later classical writer as Cicero, the Roman orator, politician and writer at the end of the republican period. Cicero devoted a long essay to the subject of old age ('De Senectute') and in it he emphasized the satisfactions of later life. Maturity of mind and insight are the natural fruits of old age, and that is why authority is put in its hands. Reminiscence is a positive asset. Far from being a sign of inability to move with the times, the past provides useful lessons. Interestingly, he attributes the disagreeable features of being old to long-standing character defects, and gives constructive advice on making the most of one's situation in later life, enjoying one's friends and using one's abilities, but without feeling one has to keep up with the pursuits of young people. Cicero's praise of old age no doubt reflects how he saw the lifestyle of his fellow senior patrician friends and colleagues.

The history of attitudes to ageing is a complex subject (Minois 1989) and it is misleading to select either positive or negative one-sided impressions of how older people were perceived in the past. The most valid generalization seems to be that western culture from the classical era to the present day has remained in a state of ambivalence in its attitudes towards old age, acknowledging both pity and respect, contempt and fear. Aristotle and Cicero exemplify very different western attitudes to ageing that have probably been present to varying degrees in many societies. It is possible to distinguish between those who have looked for and found developmental or at least adaptive changes with age, usually of an inner-directed nature, and those who have seen old age only as the negative creation of a changing bodily and social environment.

The 'Aristotelian' view predominated in much professional work with elderly people in the earlier part of this century. Ageing was seen as something to be warded off for as long as possible. This was also reflected in views on reminiscence. Rose Dobrof has written with feeling about how reminiscence used to be seen as pathological and older people were denied this means of self-expression in residential care settings in the United States (Dobrof 1984). I can remember myself visiting residential homes in London in the late 1960s and early 1970s and noting how staff frowned on the idea of encouraging reminiscence among their elderly residents. People associated reminiscing with senility, seeing only a difference of degree between a wish to reflect on and describe past events and the repetitive reminiscences of demented elderly people. We understand better now that the reason people with dementia refer so much to the past is because past memories are often clearer to them than present happenings, not because they have neglected to keep in touch with the world around them. The growth of reminiscence-based activities in the last fifteen years has been so phenomenal that it is easy to forget how different attitudes were not so long ago.

Disengagement theory

A major change in attitudes towards reminiscence began in the 1960s. The American sociologist Cowgill (1984), who has investigated the history of societal attitudes to ageing, dates the beginnings of a more positive public re-evaluation of later life to the same period. The growth of interest in reminiscence is often attributed to the writings – in fact to one article – of the American psychiatrist Robert Butler (1963). But it seems to me that a more important marker of changed ways of thinking was provided by the so-called 'disengagement theory' study, and it is worthwhile exploring the traditions of thinking within developmental psychology and functional sociology to which it belongs.

Cumming and Henry's book on ageing and disengagement was published in 1961 at the end of a large-scale, cross-sectional study of people of different ages interviewed in Kansas City. It was the first major study on ageing not to be focused on intellectual decline. In the book, Cumming and Henry argued that their data showed that people as they aged turned inwards, becoming more occupied with their own thoughts, including reminiscences about the past, and less involved in external activities and social contacts. Most importantly, older people seemed satisfied with this shift of orientation. The process of disengagement was functional for society because it encouraged younger people to take over older people's practical roles.

It is common now to malign disengagement theory. Certainly one should note how its findings may have been misused by policy makers in many countries to justify a do-nothing approach to social provision for elderly people, particularly in residential care settings, and to allow the building of sheltered housing schemes on the edge of towns, 'away in the peace and quiet', rather than close to people's previous settings. Disengagement theory was criticized also on methodological grounds, for going beyond its cross-sectional design and attempting to derive conclusions about genuine age changes rather than simply differences between generations. Subsequent investigations of the same thesis produced a much more complex set of findings. Disengagement emerged as very often forced on people by loss of social roles and disability. Many older people indeed wished to continue with an active lifestyle and were happy when this was made possible.

It is a pity, though, that the merits of disengagement theory have been lost among the many criticisms. Cumming and Henry were in fact ahead of their time in criticizing the underlying 'theory' of ageing current in American society at the time, namely that ageing is intrinsically deteriorative and successful ageing consists of looking and behaving like a middle-aged person for as long as possible. They looked respectfully for signs of developmental change in advanced age, including the tendency to reminisce. The psychological research that accompanied the main sociological study (e.g. Neugarten 1964) remains of lasting interest. This pointed to changes in personality already from middle age onwards in the individual's orientation to the inside and outside world, consistent with the views of earlier theorists such as Carl Jung. The type of research involved, which relied substantially on analysis of projective material (produced by the free play of the imagination in interpreting pictures and constructing stories), lost popularity. Psychological research in the 1960s came to focus on overt behaviour patterns and in the 1970s on underlying cognitive and rational structures to the mind. Holistic perspectives on human lives became unfashionable and have only recently re-emerged (McAdams 1990).

The power of the storyteller

In recent years, the combination of respect for intrinsic psychological change with age and the search for its social function which characterized disengagement theory has resurfaced in the developmental theory of David Gutmann. He was a member of the team that worked on the original Kansas City study, but he subsequently chose to study ageing in different traditional societies around the world. This choice was based on the cogent argument that intrinsic psychological change with age was more likely to be observed in its pure form in societies which displayed the maximum of continuity between the generations. In his book *Reclaimed Powers* (Gutmann 1987), he sets out the evidence for an ambitious theory of psychological change over the life-span, and in doing so places the kind of disengagement that he had first observed in Kansas City in a wider context.

His thesis is that in very many traditional societies, men in particular – he has a separate theory about women's development – do give up much of their 'pragmatic' power when they become old. In that sense, they disengage, but at the same time they come to take on new age-based roles. These relate to the 'sacred' power they gain as the guardians of cultural values and the mediators with the spiritual powers on whose favour the well-being of the whole society depends. As previous anthropologists (e.g. Simmons 1945) had noted, elders in various traditional societies often become the interpreters and administrators of the moral sectors of their society. They find an important social role for their reminiscences in the recounting of the myths and sacred stories on which the culture is founded, and how the society's values have been exemplified in the recent past and in their own lives. Far from being merely a reverie, a retreat from present concerns, the past is a living source of inspiration and encouragement. In Gutmann's words, 'old men help to provide young men with the powerful meanings that they require in exchange for giving up the temptations of barbarism and random procreation in favour of civility and fatherhood' (Gutmann 1987:223). Older women's greater assertiveness, he also argues, gives them an equally important enhancement of role within the extended family.

According to Gutmann, the problem for older people, and consequently for younger people as well, in modern western societies, is the progressive loss of culture which takes away these traditional roles from older people. It should be emphasized that Gutmann is no sentimental traditionalist. He recognizes that there is no going back to the type of patriarchal society that once existed. But he argues that in western societies we have lost a sense of culture, that it must be regained and that the recovery of culture and role of elderhood go hand in hand. He argues that there is a deep-rooted and reciprocally felt need on the part of older people and the rest of society for the special moral and cultural contribution that only older people can provide. It is significant, for example, that Gutmann has been sympathetic to the Grey Panthers movement in America, which has campaigned not just or principally for better services for older people, but for recovering their involvement in the life of the community. Although older people form a larger proportion of society than ever, they are more segregated from the rest of the population. Yet they have much to give. Paradoxically, Gutmann argues, this comes from their greater disengagement from ordinary daily affairs, and their longer perspective on society's history.

I have given a lot of emphasis to this recently formulated theory of older people's psychological development and social roles, and the research on disengagement from which it emerged. This is because it represents an older tradition, of ethnographic research, respectfully seeking understanding of the functions of different forms of life, which predates more recent theories on the intrapsychic functions of reminiscence. It emphasizes the place of the storyteller in traditional cultures, where reminiscence is not only enjoyable to the speaker but is also important to the hearer.

The underlying assumption to Gutmann's theory, that older people have a biological role within human society, contributing to its welfare and survival, has recently received support from research on autobiographical memory in cognitive psychology. It has been given added support by recent studies of cognitive psychologists on autobiographical memory. Graphs which record the ability of older people to recall events from their past have three clearly distinguishable elements. There is a general linear decline of memories with time which explains recent memory recall, and there is an amnesia for early childhood events which explains the absence of early memories. But there is also, in people of sufficient age, a clearly discernible bump in the graphs indicating enhanced recall of memories from the period of roughly 15–30 years of age (Rubin *et al.* 1986). Why should this be? From an evolutionary consideration it would make sense if older people could remember well events that were outside the experience of younger people. Infrequent but important occurrences, such as natural disasters, would be held better in the memory of the society.

Some sociobiologists have gone further to test hypotheses derived from an evolutionary view of older people's reminiscences, for example that older people will be more effective communicators about past events, speaking about them in a more digestible mode, and in a voice that will draw the attention of their listeners (Mergler and Goldstein 1983). These notions remain speculative at present, but at the very least they indicate a greater readiness to appreciate the social function of older people's reminiscences.

Life-review and self-preservation

The life-review and self-preservation theories are more familiar views on reminiscence and for that reason I shall refer to them relatively briefly. Both have often been cited to support the development of reminiscence work with older people, but their distinctive characters have not always been sufficiently acknowledged. As already mentioned, Robert Butler's 1963 article in a psychiatric journal is usually credited with arousing practical and research interest in reminiscence work with older people. In this paper, he outlined a theory of the 'life-review' as a normative process which all people undergo as they realize that their life is coming to an end.

Butler's article was followed by a number of other articles illustrating the psychological importance of reminiscence to older people. Another much quoted paper is that by McMahon and Rhudick (1964), who came across reminiscence apparently by chance in a study of veterans of the Spanish–American war. They noticed both how healthy and well-adjusted these old men seemed to be and how much a number of them reminisced and on this basis suggested a link between the two. Their main theoretical contribution was to point to the importance of reminiscence for maintaining a sense of identity and of self-esteem. These ideas were developed further by other researchers. In a recent book, Tobin (1991) illustrates how the capacity to make the past vivid, preferably in the presence of a sympathetic listener, can be one of the key resources very old people use in maintaining their psychological health. No conflicts may be resolved and no insights gained, but much is saved by simply allowing people to be seen as they once were and not just as they are now.

The life-review and self-preservation approaches to understanding reminiscence have in common a concern with a person's sense of identity. But whereas the latter focuses on the maintenance of worth and value in circumstances of life which may have changed drastically, the former addresses the question of the formation of an acceptable identity with which to face death. The first is directed to challenges arising from present conditions, the second to challenges from the contents of past memories themselves. This distinction is important to make also because such differently motivated reminiscences may require quite different responses from the listener. A life-review may be more rewarding but also more uncomfortable listening and the questions it throws up harder to answer.

It is the self-preservation theme which appears to lie behind most reminiscence work carried out in institutional settings, in which people are encouraged to see their life-experience as something to be valued and to be shared with others. Of course, the very term 'reminiscence' itself has positive connotations, of recall of pleasurable events, as against the 'ruminating' which may characterize a life-review. Much of the subsequent research literature that tried to establish empirically the value of reminiscence took up the theme of self-esteem maintenance and examined, for example, the relationships between spontaneous reminiscence and adjustment in elderly people undergoing relocation (Lieberman and Tobin 1983). Such comforting and encouraging reminiscence is also well suited to group settings, for example in residential homes or hospitals, and therefore feasible to include in service planning. Life-reviewing, on the other hand, requires a more individual approach, and has much more considerable resource implications. Although the idea of the life-review has become a familiar concept in the study of ageing, the potential value of life-review counselling has not yet been realized.

Empirical studies on the use of reminiscence in practice

The first research studies which sought to investigate the value of both spontaneous and provoked reminiscence produced disappointing results as reviews of the literature have indicated (Merriam 1980; Thornton and Brotchie 1987). It was commonly observed that reminiscence was enjoyed by most people, but more substantial benefits were not consistently demonstrated. One can point to methodological limitations in these studies, such as small numbers and lack of control groups. But a more significant failing was the failure of many studies to distinguish between different types of reminiscence and the different functions that thinking and talking about the past may have – life-review, identity maintenance and storytelling.

The social function of reminiscence in particular was rarely addressed. McMahon and Rhudick (1964) did refer in the course of their observations to anthropologists' descriptions of older people's storytelling role. But while they acknowledged that reminiscing could fulfil a social as well as psychological function, they attributed little importance to the former in modern society. In a published paper on a study of my own (Coleman 1974), I identified an association, among the men in my sample, between talking about important historical events in the past and drawing lessons from them and greater life satisfaction and freedom from depression. But I gave greater precedence to findings relating to the intrapsychic functions of reminiscence. The need to teach and inform by means of one's life-experience is still neglected, as studies continue to focus on reminiscence's impact on the teller without reference to the listener.

Recent studies of interventions to promote reminiscence have produced more positive results. Carefully described and controlled studies, such as Fielden's (1990) in a UK sheltered housing setting, have demonstrated the effectiveness of group reminiscence in improving well-being and socialization. As Haight (1991) has pointed out in her more recent review of predominantly

American work, early studies of one-to-one reminiscence typically evaluated the influence of interventions of very limited time duration. Outcomes were not surprisingly mixed. Indeed, all of the early studies with negative outcomes used a reminiscing intervention of one hour or less, perhaps accountable to the unsettling effects of stirring sensitive memories without follow-up. Haight's (1988) own studies have suggested that where life-review is promoted systematically over a long period of time in one-to-one interviews, the effects are uniformly beneficial. The effect of the early studies, however, was to create the impression that group reminiscing may be more therapeutic than reminiscing on an individual basis. This, however, appears to be more a reflection of length of intervention.

What investigators have learned in recent years is that research on reminiscence must do justice to the phenomenon under study as well as the intentions of any associated therapeutic intervention. More important than quantifying reminiscence activity is reaching a valid categorization of the variety of expressive and functional communications involved. In their accounts of the past, people may be explaining their actions, instructing and/or entertaining, sharing common experiences, or expressing pent-up emotions. In their internal reverie, they may be reliving past enjoyments, rethinking what might have been or reinterpreting the meaning of events (Bromley 1990).

My own research (Coleman 1986) tried to take some of these considerations into account. It was concerned with naturally occurring reminiscence, both in people's conversations and through their self-reports of thinking about the past. It was based on visits to older people living in sheltered housing schemes in London, whom I continued in many cases to visit for ten years or more. Within the material I collected, I could distinguish quite distinct sets of attitudes to reminiscence: treasuring and enjoying relating experiences; being troubled by memories of regret; seeing no point in spending time on the past; and active avoidance of thinking back because of the sense of loss it produced. This differential approach helped explain why there was no simple link between amount of reminiscence and well-being. Lack of reminiscence could also be adaptive. Much depended on the person and his or her situation. Certain types of reminiscence could fail to resolve difficulties and only increase unhappiness. Ruminating over problems without solution, for example, is not necessarily helpful. Avoidance of reminiscence may also be more purposeful if there are other more absorbing activities to turn to.

The discussion of types of reminiscing has been taken further by the Canadian psychologists Wong and Watt (1991), who distinguish six different forms: integrative, instrumental, narrative, transmissive, escapist and obsessive. Greater amounts of integrative and instrumental reminiscence characterized the better adjusted people in their study. The former conveys a sense of meaning and coherence to the life-story. The latter recalls past attempts to cope with difficult situations and thus may contribute to an enhanced subjective perception of control. The less well-adjusted people were characterized by greater amounts of obsessive reminiscence.

Disappointingly, no difference was found on the measure of use of transmissive reminiscence. But as the authors note, this could be due to the fact that:

. . . the interview setting is not an appropriate forum for transmitting personal wisdom or cultural heritage. The interviewer may be perceived as an expert or authority figure, and it is unlikely that the respondents would try to teach the interviewer a few lessons. The low prevalence of this type of reminiscence in this study is consistent with this explanation. Had we directly asked the subjects to share some of the wisdom they had acquired, the successful elderly might indeed have had more to offer.

(Wong and Watt 1991:77)

This observation highlights the importance not only of distinguishing different types of reminiscence, but also of relating them to the context in which they are being studied. We need to examine reminiscence in a variety of contexts and cultures. Much will change with the attitude of the listener.

Implications for practice

Although as a researcher I have observed people who clearly did not have any wish to reminisce or whose experience of reminiscence was painful, my own personal involvement in running and observing groups for older people has shown me the value of encouraging reminiscence. The popularity of such activity and the satisfaction gained by many of the participants is beyond question. It can also promote group cohesion as people listen respectfully to each other's individual memories and share group memories of how life used to be. Problems that have arisen have centred mainly around the logistics of running groups and securing the required staff collaboration, for example in hospital settings.

Nevertheless, comments that I have made on the uncritical use of reminiscence have been echoed by others (e.g. Adams 1987). Handbooks on the practice of encouraging reminiscence indicate the need for a greater sensitivity to different individuals' needs (Norris 1986; Gibson 1989b). In the light of the distinctions that I have already made between types of reminiscence, four points seem to be worth highlighting:

1 *Finding positive memories.* We know that adjustment to emotional upsets in life may be prolonged, indeed may never be resolved (Bromley 1990). Because they can distort the perception of other meanings, we need to tread carefully in arousing memories of these events. Certainly people should not be confronted with painful memories which are not of their choosing. For some individuals, such as psychiatric patients, large areas of the past may be dominated by traumatic experience. How then can one proceed? Lowenthal and Marrazzo (1990) describe their experience with 'milestoning', a programme they use in nursing homes for long-term psychiatric patients in which they deliberately focus on positive memories to the exclusion of negative ones. As therapists they play a directive role in stimulating and eliciting positive memories. Their work has led them to discover many childhood songs and poems which can be used to share positive memories within a group setting.

2 *Confronting painful memories.* The notion of life-review has long been mentioned as a theoretical underpinning to reminiscence work, but life-review counselling has only recently been taken seriously as a service

which we might offer to older people. Both structured discussion of the life-course and focused consideration of problem issues appear beneficial (Fry 1983; Haight 1988; Lord 1992). There is evidence of the need for opportunities for counselling in regard to disturbing memories. Surveys of elderly people coping with painful conditions highlight the negative influence of regrets about the past on the present (Walker *et al.* 1990). This area of work overlaps with spiritual counselling (Linn and Linn 1974). Both secular and pastoral counsellors need to be sensitive to the distinction between justified and unjustified self-accusations. Depressive generalizations may need to be challenged, but confessions of guilt should always be acknowledged.

It should be noted that life-reviewing also has relevance to relatively well-adjusted people. American studies demonstrate the application of individual study and groupwork to the production of integrated and rounded life-stories, and the creativity and sense of fulfilment this promotes in the participants (Kaminsky 1984; Birren and Hateley 1985).

3 *Empowering memories inhibited by grief.* An observation I have already drawn attention to from my earlier study was the refusal to reminisce on the part of those already overwhelmed by grief. Some individuals appeared to have lost so much that they could not bear to consider how happy their lives had been before. Although these reactions may seem very understandable, it is important to bear in mind that loss and griefwork are essential parts of the experience of ageing, and that older people in general are well equipped to handle grief (Gutmann 1980). They bring to the task certain strengths that they have acquired, which younger people may fail to recognize, notably a well-developed capacity to introspect (Neugarten 1988). The creation of a living inner world is a strength to respect. It may be less appropriate with an older person, whose time perspective on past and future is necessarily different, to regard the adoption of new goals and activities as the hallmark of successful adjustment to bereavement. Thinking of the deceased with sadness but without numbing pain, and with gratitude rather than regret, are better markers.

4 *Encouraging non-narcissistic memories.* People often turn to their memories not only to find comfort but also to 'boost' their sense of self-esteem in the eyes of others. Lieberman and Tobin's (1983) major study of elderly people's relocation to institutional care highlights the role of reminiscence in preserving the self, which they regard as the fundamental psychological task of late life. They criticize the life-review theory of Robert Butler for seeming to assume that people always function on the highest level of Maslow's hierarchy of needs. When it comes to psychological survival in old age, reminiscence serves more limited aims, they argue. Tobin (1989, 1991) emphasizes how important it is for residential care workers to understand this and to be more tolerant of the assertive, repetitive and ego-boosting reminiscences of the people they care for.

His comments are insightful and helpful, but need also to be set in context. Narcissistic reminiscing may be understandable but it can also be unpleasant, not only to staff but more importantly to other residents. It is reminiscing at other people's expense because its aim is not to share experience, but to claim privileged experience. Do we simply have to accept a situation where older people compete with one another to show who has been and therefore still is most important? The classical psychoanalytic model for understanding this display of power over others is that of Alfred Adler. His key concept is the sense of inferiority which people experience as children but which can be reawakened in later life by demeaning circumstances (Brink 1979). The solution according to Adler is to create *Gemeinschaftsgefuhl*, a feeling of social interest which helps transcend issues of personal significance. This again illustrates how we need to reflect more on the social significance of reminiscing, not only its interior meaning.

Reminiscence and society: culture, tradition and the public world

I would like to make this last observation the starting point for a concluding comment on the place of reminiscence and ageing within human society. We should take seriously, I think, the criticisms of those such as David Gutmann who ask what is wrong with a society that puts large numbers of older people in situations where they have to resort to anti-social behaviour to preserve their sense of self. Gutmann sees many of the pathological features associated with old age in western society (depression, anxiety, self-centredness, rigidity and mental deterioration) to be the product of loss of a meaningful role. Reminiscence should not be a means of self-defence, but of cultural support and enrichment, something that the older generation passes on to the younger.

A similar argument has been made most powerfully by Harry Moody (1984). It is recognized that reminiscence has value, but what sort of value does it have? His answer is that it lies not in the private nature of reminiscing, but in the stories themselves, and in their transformation into poetry, history and autobiography. In developing this argument, he cites two powerful analyses of contemporary culture, Christopher Lasch's (1979) *The Culture of Narcissism* and Hannah Arendt's (1958) *The Human Condition*. Lasch identifies the loss of faith in the continuity of the public world, a world beyond the self, as the main source of the modern need for self-affirmation. Traditionally, the most important consolation of old age has been the belief that future generations will in some sense carry on one's life work. When generational links begin to fray, such consolations fade. Arendt, too, identifies the intertwining of generations as the foundation of the sense of a 'common world'.

Aristotle, who opposed reminiscence to hope, was wrong. Reminiscence makes sense only if 'we believe that our memories form a continuous chain from the past into the future, from one generation to the next. Without the idea of generations we would be lost. We would live in a limbo of time made up only of passing scenes.' We are mistaken 'in thinking that people remember only for the sake of the past, when in fact old people live and remember for the sake of the future' (Manheimer 1982:98–9).

To survive, the 'common world' must be illuminated and this is achieved through older people's reminiscence and life-review:

Reminiscence, by juxtaposing past, present, and future time, helps us to recover this reverence for the public world, and here, precisely, lies the danger. If the act of reminiscence fails to recover the public world – fails, that is, to participate in something larger than a single story – then reminiscence fails of its larger purpose. In that case, reminiscence becomes merely a 'sentimental journey': an evocation of nostalgia or a flight from the present. By contrast, the old person who helps the present generation to remember the public world also redeems it from the natural ruin of time, and, for future generations, bestows guidance on the life journey. This, in its highest form, is what reminiscence and life review can mean.

(Moody 1984:161–2)

Moody is a philosopher and his writings represent an increasing and very welcome interest by scholars from the humanities in understanding human ageing (see, especially Cole *et al.* 1992). Within the social sciences, too, there is renewed interest in the understanding of whole human lives, not only in the analysis of isolated episodes and mechanisms (McAdams 1990). There is thus a common purpose to be found among psychologists, sociologists, historians, philosophers and all those interested in the study of lives, and one should look for the study of reminiscence to be increasingly enriched from these diverse sources.

They will help focus the study of reminiscing on its roots in story. The most valuable reminiscence, like the best autobiography (Abbs 1983), is that which is related to the lives of others and helps illuminate their experience too. In so doing, we also help influence their choices and behaviour, because in telling the story of our lives we describe above all our commitments, that which has given our life value. As Jerome Bruner (1991) has noted, it is for this reason that telling one's story involves the construction of one's culture not only of one's self.

2

What splendour, it all coheres: Life-review therapy with older people

JEFFREY GARLAND

Life-review therapy is defined here as a process of systematic reflection in later life, with a therapist and client trying to understand a life-history's implications for current coping strategies. Outcome is assessed in terms of resolution of conflicts, and improved well-being based on self-acceptance and having come to terms with life.

Reminiscence, of course, can be satisfying in itself without necessarily leading to psychological insight. Life-review therapy builds on reminiscence in three ways: therapist and client are committed to personal growth; the ensuing process gives particular attention to conflict resolution and the continuing evolution of coping strategies; and as therapy progresses, client and therapist note that they are not where they started. The client has become more like the person he or she really is, as outgrown defences have been examined, found wanting and laid aside.

Between reminiscence and life-review therapy, is life-review, where reminiscence is related to the present in an effort at self-evaluation akin to a form of self-therapy. Butler (1963) describes life-review as a spontaneously occurring universal mental process prompted by the realization of approaching dissolution and death, and the inability to maintain one's sense of personal invulnerability, which can result in reorganization, including achievement of wisdom, serenity and increased self-assurance.

The cultural significance of life-review has been widely recognized. For example, a striving to make sense of a life animates both popular songs such as Piaf's 'Non, je ne regrette rien' and Sinatra's 'My way', and confessional classics by Augustine and Jean-Jacques Rousseau. And the very processes which Butler viewed as characteristic of life-review – reminiscence, thinking about oneself, reconsideration of previous experiences and their meanings, and 'mirror-gazing' – can be found in psychotherapy.

Does this mean that a therapist facing a client who is ready to launch a life-review can expect that the groundwork for a therapeutic alliance will be in place? That the therapist could say with confidence: 'Not only am I boarding a moving bus, but my client the driver and I will be in agreement on the route and destination?' This is not necessarily the case, as we shall see in examining the concept of life-review, and the range of its therapeutic and other functions.

The status of life-review therapy

Life-review is a pervasive theme in psychotherapies which work towards a client achieving 'insight' in developing a more varied and useful set of models for the interpretation and understanding of experience. As Knight (1986:127–8) points out: 'In a certain sense, all psychotherapy involves some elements of life review as a component of understanding oneself and effecting change by releasing old unresolved conflicts.'

A breakthrough of insight in life-review therapy is an intense experience for client and therapist. Both could echo the shout of Herakles illuminated in fire: 'What splendour, it all coheres' (Pound 1956). It is understandable, therefore, that therapists were excited in 1963 when Butler reaffirmed the significance of life-review. Dobrof (1984b:xviii) recalls:

> In a profound sense, Butler's writings liberated both the old and the nurses, doctors and social workers; the old were free to remember . . . And we were free to listen, and treat rememberers and remembrance with the respect they deserved.

Kastenbaum (1987) is more circumspect, offering the wry comment that one of the attractions of life-review is to put ageing in a positive light in a culture where reflection tends to be undervalued, and to be thought positively un-American. On balance, though, life-review has received more criticism than commendation in the literature on psychotherapy for older people. Knight (1986:124–5) warns:

> The phrase 'life review' has become a kind of buzzword that is used to cover a wide variety of activities. Interventions range from the simple suggestions that old people need not necessarily be interrupted when they reminisce through the intermediate suggestion that the professional listen to the elder and attempt to understand what is said, up to theory-based psychotherapeutic intervention.

Kastenbaum (1987:325) reinforces this point:

> It is difficult to evaluate life-review oriented intervention and prevention strategies for many reasons; perhaps the most troublesome is the lack of clear distinction between life review *per se* and the variety of other retrospective modalities employed by adults of all ages.

For Karpf (1982), life-review therapy is an environmental modification, a supportive technique rather than an interpretative one: 'The optimism of Butler and his colleagues is infectious but it strays far afield of what many would consider psychotherapy' (p. 26).

Edinberg (1985) notes that while life-review therapy encourages clients to 'get their life in order' and is a flexible approach which can be tailored to individual or group, it should be criticized for (1) a lack of clarity on how to apply procedures, (2) over-reliance on clinical judgement of how to use it, (3) little scientific validity, (4) limited utility in handling specific problems (such as adapting to organic dysfunction) and (5) a lack of clarity about how this therapy might benefit persons with reactive depression, or conflict with other therapies.

A constructive suggestion which could contribute to addressing some of these points is offered by Molinari and Reichlin (1985). They distinguish three types of reminiscence: storytelling, evaluating experience and defensive (against an ungratifying present). Confining life-review therapy to the second category, and noting the potential for conflict if unresolved failures, disappointments or losses are encountered, they recommend that a more circumscribed and workable version of Butler's life-review is needed for its validity to be on a sound footing. They do not elaborate this idea directly, but their line of argument appears to imply that life-review therapy, to be a distinctive way of using reminiscence, should be direct in evaluating experience, with the client avoiding as far as possible storytelling and defensiveness.

How life-review therapy can help older people

Reminiscence in its various guises can function as a pastime, as a form of self-therapy, or as part of a life-review shared with a therapist. Edinberg (1985) sees life-review as having a 'multifaced' role: 'to aid the client in achieving new insight (and resultant peace of mind); to put closure on troublesome events from the past; to view earlier events from a new perspective; and to help rekindle lost skills or abilities' (p. 160). With such versatility, life-review therapy could be a real gem. However, the history of psychotherapy, like a Ratner's sale, is littered with items of bright promise that disappoint on closer examination. A careful appraisal is needed before we can be sure of the value of this therapy.

Three main interrelated functions appear to have been described in the literature. These relate to the client's subjective experience and involve the enhancement of the individual's feeling of: being in control of one's own life; understanding of self in relation to others; and enjoyment of life.

Brink (1979:181) advises an Adlerian perspective on control:

> The life review, when it is helpful, is helpful because it has reminded the patient that life is a series of crises and protracted struggles, and that he has persevered in the past and triumphed. Such an interpretation of one's past serves as a powerful motivation for one to try to cope with the new demands of the present. When the therapist debriefs the patient on his autobiography, the therapist must emphasize enthusiastically this interpretation of the patient's life.

This echoes a theme developed by Goldfarb and Turner (1953), concerning their perception of a need for older patients to feel powerful and in control during the process of psychotherapy when confronting an authority figure in the person of the therapist.

Narration confers spell-binding power on older people, as witness the wise women or wizards of tales and legends who relate secrets and propound riddles, and in more recent imagery Coleridge's Ancient Mariner, and another teller of tall stories, the old sailor shown in the painting 'The Boyhood of Raleigh'. Social anthropologists have indicated that across a wide range of cultures the status of old people is positively related to the amount of worthwhile information they have to impart. In emphasizing the client's storytelling, framing and reframing personal meaning, as the core of therapeutic process, life-review therapy could be said to share with other reminiscence-based activities the characteristic of empowering older people.

Lewis and Butler (1974) view older people who use life-review spontaneously without a therapist as mediator as attempting to gain control of fear of approaching death. Life-review, they suggest, is entered as a refuge, as a person's myths of immortality and invulnerability give way. They propose that the newly vulnerable individual be seen as engaging in life-review as a reflex bid to regain control. Sometimes this represents a self-styled certificate of sanity, as was the case with an eighty-year-old client listening to my summary of his life-review as 'a man of letters – an artist', and exulting: 'This will tell 'em I'm still *compos mentis.*'

Like a comfort blanket, life-review confers a sense of control via security. Verwoerdt (1988) points out that its purpose is not necessarily accurate recall of facts, but the weaving of edited recollections into a harmonious perspective, constructing an alternative reality ego syntonic (compatible) with self-esteem. As Nietzsche reminds us, when Memory and Pride have a battle to debate an event in a person's life-story, Pride usually wins.

Indeed, Lieberman and Tobin (1983) consider that most people do not have the ability to undertake unaided the comprehensive and balanced sorting and restructuring of the past envisaged by Jung or Erikson. They appear to consider that rather than aspiring to be an architect redesigning the psyche, the ordinary person's best efforts at self-analysis will resemble the bodging of a cowboy builder. Lieberman and Tobin see as an essential task of old age the preservation of a coherent, consistent self in the face of loss and the threat of loss, but suggest that because human resources are so scanty and the task is so pressing, life-review primarily is used to create an image intended to be believed, a myth to achieve a feeling of stability, justifying the narrator's life. For them, typically, the older person becomes the protagonist in a drama that is worth telling or having lived for.

Awareness is needed in life-review therapy of a client's omissions or distortions, such as talking about one parent but never mentioning the other, or 'glorifying' a spouse or child (Edinberg 1985), and it must be recognized that in the interest of reducing cognitive dissonance, fact and fantasy can mingle in life-review (Lewis, 1973).

While not in a legalistic sense insisting on the truth and nothing but the truth, the therapist needs to help the client challenge major distortions. For example, I had to take a very depressed woman of eighty-two, convinced that nothing good had ever happened in her life, back to the age of eight. Her parents had a corner shop in Cardiff open all hours, and were celebrating a good week's takings. They gave her a few pence to get some fish and chips for herself – a rare treat. She shared the food in the rain under a street light, 'with my friend – she had a squint and she was smelly but she was my friend – and I was happy'. Having overturned the depressive's first commandment (you can have any colour you like, so long as it's black), we were able to move on to recognize other times in her life when she had been happy, and to plan how such feelings could be regained.

A second popular perspective is of life-review therapy as a cognitive map, or at least an orienteering aid, to help the client achieve a more insightful understanding of self in relation to others as a developmental goal of late life. A well-known formulation set out by Erikson (1950) is resolution as a choice between Ego Integrity *vs* Despair. Identifying an overriding need for older people to attempt to make sense of present experience in the context of the past, Erikson sees integrity as a positive 'acceptance of one's one and only life cycle as something that has to be and that by necessity permitted of no substitutions' (p. 268).

Coleman (1986) is not alone in noting that close similarities can be detected between the concept of a normative life-review and Erikson's notion of the developmental task of achieving integrity. However, Butler (1975) might have found this parallel difficult to follow, as he appears dismissive of Erikson:

> His experience with the middle aged and elderly is very meager, and his popular conceptions of generativity versus stagnation and integrity versus despair do not hold up well in my clinical and research experience with patients in middle and later life.
>
> (Butler 1975:255)

Possibly Butler might have found it easier to accept a comparison between life-review and the Jungian framework of individuation seen as a developmental theme for the second half of life, a rounding out of the whole person (Jung 1933). Jung's view of individuation is evoked by Lewis and Butler (1974:165) when they write: 'The older person reflects in order to resolve, reorganise and reintegrate what is troubling or preoccupying him.' These authors point out that a therapist would deal with life-review essentially to facilitate an older person's ongoing self-analysis, making it more conscious, deliberate and efficient, supporting rather than supplanting what has been happening. And Edinberg (1985:160) notes that therapy 'should be developed around whatever type of analysis of previous events the client is doing'.

The theme of learning is taken up by a number of authors. Knight (1986) makes the point that even if we do not concede that there are typical developmental changes in adult life, we could consider life-review as taking in the learning of age-graded roles rather than personality change as such; learning of this kind could still be problematic and stressful and an issue for therapy. Discussing the habitual mirror gazing noted by Butler (1963) as characterizing some presentations of the life process, Kimmel (1990) proposes that this represents the person actively learning to integrate a changing physical 'me' into the relatively continuous sense of 'self' in an attempt to integrate experience on the basis of current functioning.

Molinari and Reichlin (1985) see life-review in terms of mourning with stages encompassing: reorganization of relationship to lost other; obsessive recounting and reiteration; reflection on self-absorption; and the end result, learning to relinquish what has been lost. Such tidy phrases can conceal a frenetic struggle by a client who is 'hanging on like grim death' to a lost other. I recall engaging in life-review therapy with a woman widowed two years before when her 'devoted' husband stepped out of line for once by going for a walk by himself, against her wishes. (She had been unwell and had hoped he would have stayed to keep her company.) On the walk he was knocked down by a bus, and died from his injuries. She reacted with extreme and enduring guilt, but would not confront directly her anger at her husband for having gone against her wishes, and having had the last word as he left the house. Red-faced and with veins standing out on her forehead, she proclaimed: 'I blame the bus company. I blame the surgeons. I blame God. But angry with him? Me?'

A third dimension to life-review therapy concerns increased enjoyment of life for the client, who can find it an intrinsically satisfying process, quite apart from any gain in perceived control over one's life or greater understanding of self in relation to others. Some of my clients have likened the 'feel' of life-review therapy to pulling on 'old faithful' slippers and automatically feeling more comfortable and relaxed about oneself. Others have reported a heady sensation akin to putting on dancing shoes to 'strut your stuff', and it is not uncommon for such clients to break into song during therapy or to illustrate feelings with dance steps.

Comfort is commented on by Kiernat (1984), reporting groupwork in which members identifying themselves as having had an impoverished childhood were encouraged to use reminiscence to enhance their appreciation of the present. And a sense of life as dance is evoked by Lewis and Butler (1974), discussing the experience of 'elementality' in life-review: 'The lively capacity to live in the present may be fostered through the enjoyment of people, nature, colours, love, humour, and beauty in any form' (p. 168). They report older people rapt with reminiscent intensity: 'I felt as though I was there', or 'it's as though it only happened yesterday'.

In this mix of observation and speculation, recurrent themes of control, insight and enjoyment can be identified, but little or nothing appears to have been written on how these interrelate, or on their relative priority in different situations. Verwoerdt (1988), though, does draw our attention to the possibility of a two-dimensional model for the life-review process. He describes an account of a self-chosen twelve-month retreat in the mountains by a 65-year-old man who wrote down his thoughts and impressions from day to day. At first the journal was a convergent 'vertical' record of autobiographical material involving concentration, memory and logical thought. Then, gradually, 'horizontal' impressionistic thoughts reflecting fleeting observations, playful and using free association, began to emerge, and during the last six months became more dominant.

This resembles a cycle which I have found characteristic of clients in life-review therapy. In some phases of therapy, assurance of being in control of one's own life becomes the salient issue: themes of responsibility, of intention, of self-efficacy and purpose are elaborated. The client declares: 'I may be stubborn . . . difficult . . . bloody-minded . . . but I am not going to be pushed around . . . taken for granted . . . just used by other people.' In this mode strategic phrases abound: 'I thought to myself . . . I made up my mind . . . it was time for me to have a say in what happened.' In other phases the client turns, sometimes spontaneously, sometimes with a nudge from me, to expressing a need to understand the thoughts and actions they have described, in terms of their implications for self-esteem and relationships. Self-expression tends to be more idiosyncratic, discursive and fragmentary: 'It sank in then . . . I get the message . . . it really hits me . . . so that's what it's all about.'

In my experience of life-review therapy, modes tend to alternate within sessions like contrasting segments of a Gestalt pattern in which 'figure' and 'ground' vie for attention. The client (or therapist) who becomes fixated on the issue of being in charge of one's own life may well risk premature termination of therapy, settling for being safe rather than sorry. If the search for understanding self in relation to others becomes the mode of fixation, the client (or therapist) can become overly concerned with putting two and two together, irrespective of the answer. Flexible movement between and balance among these modes can determine success in therapy.

Methods of life-review therapy

Much more has been written on the theory of this therapy than on its practicalities. For example, as a practitioner, I have become aware of the importance of selectively amplifying early events that the client recalls with particular clarity, highlighting key phrases that are most salient in an individual life-review, challenging as vigorously as possible 'if only . . .' sidetracking, and working with the client on the interpretation of unresolved dreams recurring from early life.

A current client, a 69-year-old woman marooned in an old people's home by the effects of a severe stroke, recalls that when as a child she had finished a drink she threw the glass to the floor: 'I thought that if I had finished drinking from it, it was no good to me any more. My mother used to say that I cost her a fortune in glasses!' In relating her history, she repeats: 'I wasn't born with a silver spoon in my mouth!' Exploring such utterances, to illuminate her current experience of battling to force hard-pressed care staff to satisfy her needs before those of other residents, has become pivotal for our shared efforts to bring about a situation in which resident and staff can meet each other half-way.

The above client has no time for 'if only . . .'. Very different, at the start of therapy, was another client, a 74-year-old widow, emerging from the shadows of a 52-year marriage to a self-styled 'long-standing anxiety neurotic'. In the early stages of bereavement, she became preoccupied with self-blame: if only she had been stronger perhaps he would have become strong; if only she had known how to bring him back from his withdrawn moods, and how to stand up to the emotional blackmail of his threats to kill himself; if only she had taken note of warning signs of his character during their engagement . . .

Therapy focused on recognition of the inevitability of their lives, and enabled her to question the usefulness of hanging on to 'if only'. At the start of this process, she often returned to highlighting her 'foolishness' for having clung to 'if only', using this self-criticism as another stick to beat herself with. It was necessary, using a range of tactics, to keep returning her to the issue of how she could integrate her insights in a pragmatic way, looking for what was useful to her, rather than expending valuable energy in self-blame, and in continuing to choose to spend her life on self-wounding regret.

Discussing her difficulty in using new-found freedom, the client recounted the return of nightmare from childhood. She approached 'a dark tunnel, where some savage beast like a lion or maybe a tiger was cooped up'. She woke in terror as the beast was about to be released. We re-enacted the dream using Gestalt therapy in which the dreamer re-lives the dream to encounter the feared object as a split-off and disowned part of herself which needs to be understood, accepted and re-integrated in a more assertive lifestyle. As the client expressed it: 'I've really got to dig my claws in – hard!' As Brink (1979:210) acknowledges, life-review is facilitated by 'dreams that affirm the richness of one's life, or one's link to the past or future'.

I have also found guided imagery exercises particularly helpful for clients who have difficulty in 'switching on' to life-review. I ask them to describe in words or any other medium of their choice, with themes selected to reflect individual interests, their life 'as if' it were a house or a garden, a knitting pattern or a Pools coupon, a pub or a party, and to proceed to fill the space with a vivid picture of life-experience.

Attempts to standardize administration of life-review are of comparatively recent origin (Haight 1992). In most cases, a variety of approaches is used, with Lewis and Butler (1974) listing: written or taped autobiographies, with feedback that may include self-confrontation in a mirror, listening to tapes and picking up areas of conflict, boring and repetitive elements; pilgrimages; reunions, geneaology; scrapbooks, photo albums, old letters and memorabilia; summation of life work; and exercises in preserving ethnic identity. Music should be added to this list: as Bazant (1992) points out, it is a rich resource. Chubon (1980) introduces the theme of relating to a novel, reporting a case history in which a client was prescribed the reading of a novel with several similarities to her own life, reviewing the book in relation to her life in subsequent counselling.

Greene (1982) shows that a family dimension may be built in, reporting a case study of a daughter encouraged to be present at her father's life-review and to respond to content bearing on their relationship. And Mouratoglou (1991:13) notes family therapists with older couples can:

> feedback to each partner the story of their lives since childhood. Those stories verbalise agreements and interpretations accepted between individuals and their current families as well as their families of origin. Such stories are followed up by articulations of the couple's current dilemmas regarding changes in their contract and by setting up tasks for them to experience the impact of new rules/agreements.

Groupwork in the context of sharing general and historical topics of reminiscence is a distinctive area of diversionary activity. Intense personal reminiscence shading into life-review is an important strand in the process of group therapy and such groups can offer a more accessible way of developing insight into self in relation to others. Lesser *et al.* (1981) note that when a member begins individual life-review, the group's reaction is to put together a synthesis of legend around such themes as first memory, first day at school or first dating experience. The value of peer support is urged by Brink (1979), who advises that: 'The group must be structured so that the patient will receive positive reinforcement for recounts of effective coping, and nonreinforcement (but supportive encouragement) for ineffective coping' (p. 324).

Some issues in life-review

A therapy is not a panacea: for both client and therapist it is important to be selective, weighing the pros and cons of a proposed approach before reaching an informed decision. As Kastenbaum (1987:325) asks: 'under what circumstances . . . is life review a valuable form of prevention, and under what circumstances is it useless or potentially harmful?' Brink appears to suggest that as is the case with many therapies, the least affected clients may show most gain. He considers: 'When the patient has been successful in meeting life's problems, a life review is a good tactic' (p. 182). Edinberg (1985:161) recommends life-review therapy for:

> Clients who have sufficient verbal skills and cognitive ability both to recall previous events and achieve some insight into them. It is also aimed at persons who have had enough positive experiences in life so that the life review will not be a depressing experience.

Description of contraindications for life-review therapy has attracted a little more attention in the literature. Lewis and Butler (1974) recognize that some older people prefer to carry out a solo life-review and would resent a therapist's attention. For Coleman (1986), too, life-review can be a private matter, as: 'People do not necessarily want or benefit from the help of a counsellor on "putting their house in order"' (p. 156). Verwoerdt (1988) reminds us, though, that life-review is intimately related to the notion of what one is and has been for others. A need for forgiveness and reconciliation may be felt, and the most direct way of meeting this would be to involve another. Brink (1979:193) advises against life-review therapy: 'In patients whose lives and memories are, on the balance, unsuccessful and painful.'

Should persons with dementia be excluded from this therapy? Lewis and Butler view brain damage as not necessarily a contraindication. Woods *et al.* (1992:159) conclude: 'Life reviews . . . can be conducted with elderly persons with dementia', but the studies they report appear to deal with life-review presented as general reminiscence 'activity' and 'care-giving'.

Evaluation of the effects of life-review therapy is a matter of increasing concern. As my own therapeutic approach is one of reasoned eclecticism, using life-review only where necessary to meet a client's expressed needs and invariably in conjunction with a variety of other techniques as appropriate, I can only report that when clients are asked at the conclusion of my intervention to evaluate the usefulness of the different components they experienced, life-review consistently receives a high rating.

Negative outcomes occasionally are acknowledged as possible, but they do not appear to be recorded in the literature. Lewis and Butler (1974) describe as possible outcomes of life-review therapy, regret, anxiety, guilt, despair and depression, but it is not clear to what extent, if at all, they experienced their patients as responding in these ways. They caution that the individual may become terror-stricken and even suicidal, concluding prematurely and without reference to the therapist that life has been a total waste, but they do not indicate how frequent such a termination is in their experience. Similarly, Verwoerdt (1988) notes that the results of life-review may range from nostalgia to severe depression with suicidal tendencies, without indicating the proportion of cases he has encountered at the negative end of this spectrum. Kastenbaum (1987) also talks in general terms about the risk of encouraging life-review in an 'obsessive' older person given to undue self-reflection, but does not give evidence for his misgivings.

The effectiveness of reminiscence activities in general has been questioned by Thornton and Brotchie (1987). Until recently, evidence for the usefulness of life-review therapy has been confined to single case reports. One of the most noteworthy of these is an account by Frankl (1973) of a single session on a hospital ward with a patient aged eighty dying of cancer. A former cleaner, she had brought up a family in a life of unremitting toil. Now she was depressed, withdrawn and scared of death. Frankl asked her: 'What do you think when you look back at your life? Has life been worth living?' His intention was to help the patient to bless her own life, to say 'yes' to life despite everything. He told her at the end of their interview, 'No one can blot out what has happened to you. No one can blot out your courage in suffering now. Your life is a great achievement and accomplishment. I congratulate you.' The patient died not long after, but she had become transformed, working to help other patients as Frankl had helped her.

One of the most recent references to single case success is by Wasylenki (1989), working with a businessman whose sexual dysfunction was alleviated following life-review therapy focusing on the evolution of his sexual identity.

Sustained and successful effort to demonstrate significant gains in life satisfaction following life-review is reported by Haight, summarizing three studies carried out over six years. The process involved a series of six one-hour counselling interviews based on her own life-review and experiencing form (LREF) and (before and after counselling) completion of the Life Satisfaction Index-A (LSI-A) (Neugarten *et al.* 1961). In all studies, an experimental group received life-review, while a control group had friendly visits without life-review. The third study added a 'no-treatment' group receiving pre- and post-tests only. Each of the studies was of a different population: 'elderly people in good health in the community'; 'veterans residing in a nursing home'; and participants who 'all . . . were physically disabled in some way and depended on "at-home services" to live independently in the community' (pp. 284–5). The average age of the subjects was seventy-four years in the first two studies and seventy-six in the third. In each, significant positive gains in life-satisfaction were found with life-review, while the controls showed non-significant negative changes.

While these are some encouraging indicators, it is clear that life-review therapy needs a more substantial foundation of research findings. Molinari and Reichlin's questions are still waiting from 1985. What is the optimal time, ideal frequency of sessions, type of content? What processes lead to what kind of positive (or negative) outcome? What older people can benefit? Does the nature of life-review vary according to age? How is life-review experienced from the client's perspective? How does life-review affect reactions to ongoing problems?

While all these questions raise important issues, perhaps priority should be given to linking the last two, evaluating outcome with subjective and objective criteria. In view of the shortage of therapists working one-to-one with older people, such a programme might include comparison of outcome for: group and individual therapy; experienced therapists, trainees and clients' peers as facilitators; or a co-counselling approach in which pairs of older people alternate life-review, exchanging roles of narrator and auditor, with conventional client–therapist life-review therapy.

Conclusions

While a spontaneous life-review takes the form of a journey of self-analysis, this does not necessarily mean that everyone setting out on a life-review will be willing or able to enter or complete life-review therapy. Out of choice or necessity the process may not involve a therapist, or may be aborted for a variety of reasons, as there are many threats and distractions in any pilgrim's progress. Life-review has its splendours but also its miseries for the alienated individual who finds the struggle to confront existential isolation painful, and sometimes unendurable.

Life-review is a component of many therapeutic approaches, and perhaps because it is so embedded specific investigation of its efficacy has been relatively neglected. It appears that the main functions of successful life-review therapy for the client are enhancement of: a sense of being in control of one's own life; understanding self in relation to others; and enjoyment of life.

As Kastenbaum (1987) recommends, professionals working with life-review need to give more critical attention to basic assumptions and to testing the effectiveness of differentiated applications. There are a few encouraging signs that evidence is being collected in response to his challenge that with life-review, '. . . clinical gerontology has let itself be carried away by the best of intentions – seizing upon a positive idea and rushing it into practice without careful evaluation and without even seeming to recognize the need for such evaluation' (p. 325).

Clinicians and researchers need to come together to ensure that the splendid opportunities offered by life-review therapy are extended more effectively to the client's advantage. Using qualitative analysis and working in a much closer partnership with each other and with the clients themselves (whose contribution to devising methods of evaluation has been sadly neglected), we need to face three related challenges: (1) to refine life-review therapy so that it becomes more coherent and focused; (2) to investigate outcomes from the client's viewpoint; and (3) to carry out a controlled study of the effects of one-to-one therapy in comparison with group therapy, peer counselling, and other cost-effective approaches. We need, though, to do this in a balanced way, gaining discipline without crushing vitality. We should remember the story of God and the Devil out for a walk together. God finds a beautiful shining object in their path and picks it up. The Devil fails to recognize it. Perhaps he is dazzled by the unpredictable flashes of light that dart from its many facets. Certainly his curiosity is aroused. 'What's that?' he asks eagerly. 'This?' says God. 'This is Truth'. 'Ah!' says the Devil, uncomprehending, 'Here – give it to me! Let me *organize* it for you.'

3

An interesting confusion:
What can we do with reminiscence
groupwork?

MIKE BENDER

For the past ten years, I have led or supervised a number of reminiscence groups with different types of clients and for different purposes. Between 1982 and 1988, I headed a team of applied psychologists working in a Social Services Department in the East End of London, providing services to all client groups. Then, in 1988, I moved to a Health Authority in the South West to work full-time in services for older people, although I have continued my interest in the use of reminiscence work with people with learning difficulties.

This experience has led me to consider three basic issues which reminiscence groupwork raises for me: What is its range of usefulness and what purposes can it serve? What is its relationship to mainstream psychotherapy? And, what is its standing as a therapeutic method?

In this chapter, I describe the work I have been involved in and draw out points which I feel go some way towards answering these questions. In the interests of coherence, I have chunked the chronology into various stages. The actual experience, of course, was not so neatly packaged!

In 1981, I went to visit Neville Marston at the Social Services Department, Northampton. He was one of the unsung pioneers of applied psychology for older people – group living, cook/chill foods, etc. – and he showed me proudly round some homes where there was one definite activity going on each day. I decided to see if I could help a home organize two activities a day. Muriel Johns, an officer-in-charge, was happy to set this up but asked, not unreasonably, which group was I going to run? This had not been on my agenda, so picking this month's flavour out of the air, I said I'd run a reminiscence group.

I'd never run one, but since another clinical psychologist, Andrew Norris, had popularized such groups (Norris 1986), and since one clinical psychologist is supposed to do everything another one can, I could hardly back down. So I went off to find someone to share the problem, and in this way, Paulette Bauckham – the Leisure Organizer – and I started running reminiscence groups in old people's homes. We had no particular therapeutic intent. We just couldn't bear to see the residents sitting in the lounge day after day.

We handed the purpose and selection of the group members over to the officer-in-charge and a clinical psychologist, Alison Cooper. They selected a rather difficult group, six withdrawn residents – 'wallflowers'. Such an approach is quite contrary to the advice we were later to give in *Groupwork with the Elderly* (Bender *et al.* 1987), where we stressed the importance of 'winning with your first group' by gradually building up your competence and confidence. It took us a number of sessions to 'thaw' the members out a bit but, when we did, they enjoyed the sessions so much that we didn't have the heart to stop the group and added another four sessions to the original eight. There was also a second issue that concerned us: a lady who talking about her father kept shaking her head and saying what a bastard he was. We were at a bit of a loss as to what to do. We didn't know whether to encourage her to explain her very strong feelings more fully. Could the group take it? Or should we quietly discourage her, which seemed coercive? After about the third time this happened, it seemed sensible to get some supervision, so Paulette and I headed up to Fulbourne Hospital, Cambridge, to discuss the group with Andrew Norris.

I came away with two useful ideas. First, where a person is displaying a strong emotion, it always pays to ask the group members if they have had similar experiences. In this way, you gain the information needed to gauge whether the group is able to take the issue on board at that stage of its development; and given the group leader's respect for the members' ability, the members have a structure within which to feel secure to look at difficult issues. It is rare that they will then not do so. In this case, maltreatment by parents was something the group could handle quite securely, with the concomitant expression of strong emotions. And, although of course they did not remark on it – one must never underestimate how polite older people in our welfare services are – we thought that they were probably glad that, at last, the group leaders had the confidence to tackle the issue and let it be aired.

There was another issued raised at that supervision session with Andrew. We felt terrible at the idea of ending the group. The idea of returning the members to their chairs filled us with reluctance and guilt. I term this 'taking on the guilt of the world', taking responsibility for all the insults and injuries done to our clients. Understanding that you can't doesn't always make not doing it easier; but to take on that guilt is to doom yourself to a certain burnout.

With any group, you need to bear in mind the well-being of the members after the group ends: What do they want to happen? What problems still require help? Can the group usefully continue? In what form? And you need to have these questions in mind long before the group ends; as a rule of thumb, from half-way through the life of the group.

We made one important innovation. Our members had been chosen because they were shy, withdrawn people. This made for slow development of communication between members in the session. To encourage the process, we decided to arrange for two tables to be put together, so that they could all sit together at mealtimes. We had to wade through a load of reasons against such a radical change – people would fall over the two tables (there was actually plenty of space); cook had a list of diabetics by table (a complete fiction), etc. – but eventually, it was agreed and the effect was amazing. Within a session or two, the whole morale of the group was raised, and they were talking to each other not just to us, so it was much easier for us to close the group after twelve sessions.

We then decided to see if we could use reminiscence groupwork for all the main types of residents found in the authority's residential homes. We never selected or assessed. The matron of a home who wanted our involvement was given some indication of the type of group we wanted to run and she selected the members. For example, a visually handicapped group did well when we ran it; but we made the mistake of handing it over to two staff who, although we supervised them, did not transmit an atmosphere of respect. The mistake here was not to leave one of us behind to co-lead and model good leadership.

A hard-of-hearing group used a 'loop' which allowed direct transmission from a central, mobile microphone to their hearing aid. Only one person at a time could speak into this microphone, but this did not prove to be a problem and it become a lovely group. These members were so grateful and pleased to be able to communicate clearly. Within a short while, they had formed a club which required little staff input. They met regularly, planned their own events and invited hard-of-hearing residents from other homes to their group. This was an excellent example of using reminiscence groupwork as a means to an end. Cohesion and trust between members build up as the group develops, and gives them a collective self-confidence which they can use for another task.

One of the most bizarre assignments we undertook was a reminiscence group in a home where the officer-in-charge had accommodated all her difficult residents in one corridor and when they, not surprisingly, got on badly, called us in to run a group for them. It failed because of our lack of technique. Two residents – a man and a woman – spent most of the first sessions insulting each other. We tried to impose external solutions. We should have given the problem to the group to sort out. They might have banned one or both of the quarrellers. I don't know what they would have decided but *the wisdom is in the group*; if the other members had wanted what we had to offer, you can be sure they would have sorted out the difficulties.

Paulette and I had long been concerned that residents got out of their homes too rarely, and we got the idea of a 'leisurely luncheon club' at the local psychiatric day-centre. So half a dozen residents walked or had their wheelchairs pushed to the day-centre, where for an hour they shared a gentle reminiscence group with some of the longer-term psychiatric clients who were, of course, rather younger; however, age is not an important determinant of success in a reminiscence group. Then they had lunch and, after coffee, came home. Once we had sorted out the administrative arrangements, the group ran for a long time.

Naturally, Paulette and I wanted to create a body of enthusiastic reminiscence groupworkers and undertook quite a bit of training of residential care assistants, which formed the basis for *Groupwork with the Elderly* (Bender *et al.* 1987); but, sadly, after I left, reminiscence groupwork in the homes gradually stopped, despite Paulette's efforts. However, in 1990, she created a reminiscence centre in a disused lounge of an old people's home – recreating the kitchen and sitting room of a 1930s East End home. Groups of residents are bussed to this centre most days of the week and, it would appear, many enjoy the experience.

Can reminiscence groupwork be of use to people with learning difficulties?

In 1987, I decided to spend some time seeing if reminiscence groupwork could be usefully offered to people with severe learning difficulties. It seemed clear to me that it might be useful to provide such clients with an identity based on their geography and history. So with Val Levens, a speech therapist, I ran a variety of short groups (four to eight sessions) – they were short because I didn't know when I was leaving my post. However, such a small number of sessions is unsuitable for people with a learning difficulty; I would now probably offer them a ten-session group, to be renewed (probably, after a short break) if that was what they wanted when they evaluated the group in the ninth session. I would also use this evaluation to review whether all the members should continue in the group or not; however, it is important to realize that terminating a person's membership of the group sends a strong message of leader power throughout the group, which leads to anxiety, uncertainty and feelings of powerlessness. Termination of membership should therefore not be undertaken without careful thought as to the likely effects.

Having decided on a theme for a group, we would then run two groups – one for people with medium disability and one for people with severe disability. All we hoped to show in these groups was that we could provide stimuli (slides, sounds, objects) that engaged them, so that they paid attention and didn't get bored or wander off. In fact, it was during these sessions that we got unexpected therapeutic effects: group members' verbal ability improved and they were able to clearly express very strong emotions, especially regarding loss; they also showed self-control and patience that was quite contrary to what staff reported their usual behaviour to be like.

There was one other very strong impression left from those groups. Val and I were working with some of the most difficult people in the day-centre. Quite a few had been sent to residential units which specialized in behavioural problems. In our groups, there was no aggression, or shouting, or in fact any socially unacceptable behaviour. Yet when I saw them around the day-centre, their behaviour was far worse and the staff were confrontational and devaluing – the two were obviously linked. Some staff resented groupwork when it took other staff off the floor, despite the fact that they had very little to offer except mindless industrial work. Indeed, our members would have been foolish to express their vulnerabilities and to try to apply what they were learning with us in terms of self-respect and agency outside the group.

One young man illustrated this all too clearly. He had shown aggression in his residential unit and in the day-centre but showed none at all in our group. He had very limited verbal ability but had taken an active part in the group we led on family life, and had attended, focused and answered to the best of his ability. Given verbal IQ subtests in the follow up, he acted completely blank with the simplest question. It was as if he had retreated into playing the 'dumb subbie'; but I had seen him functioning at a much higher level in the group.

This experience is identical to that reported by Sinason (1992) in her psychotherapeutic work.

As we set up the various groups, we left the *Recall* pack behind. In my opinion, although it is useful if the group's aim is stimulation, and it is a useful learning situation for inexperienced group leaders, the slide-tape pack tends to dictate what is talked about. Using a projector means the group never sits in a circle, which is important in encouraging member–member communication. However, most important, it allows members to retreat from the complexity of their private feelings into well-practised roles of 'cheerful chappies (and gals)'.

The groups I had run with Val had left me with the idea that reminiscence groupwork could help develop a sense of identity among people with learning difficulties, who had been born in the same area around the same time. The old area of Plymouth, to which I had by then moved, is the Barbican. So I thought I would run a 'Born on the Barbican' group – a catchy title provides a purpose and focus to a group, which other staff can quickly pick up. However, West Devon Social Services is divided into teams serving geographical districts and, when I eventually found a co-leader, Fran Seeley, she told me the group would have to be called 'Born in St. Budeaux and Honicknowle', which didn't have quite the same ring. So we ran a group exploring the experience of living in a mental handicap hospital; this unearthed some pretty traumatic memories. I also had come to appreciate the need for regular supervision even more strongly than previously. We had weekly supervision sessions with Ron Wood, an experienced clinical psychologist, which were a great help with this group.

We used one of the sessions of this group to visit the site of the mental hospital. It had been demolished, but the church where the more able attended every Sunday was still there; the patients sat in the back rows, a neat positional statement of their inferiority. One of the group members wandered carefully around the church, relishing her new found freedom and then stood behind the lectern for a few minutes as if reading a lesson. If she had been properly valued and educated, I'm sure she could have done so.

This group ran for eight sessions and Fran felt strongly that such a group should be renewable, at the wishes of its members. I therefore ran another such group in a centre for people with learning difficulties who were over sixty-five and the group had the right to negotiate more sessions. What went wrong with this group was that some of its members did not have the ability to verbalize their experiences; and, for the first time, I felt it would have been better to select so that there was a similar range of verbal abilities and speed of speech in the group. The average verbal ability of this group was much lower than that of the group of ex-inmates I had run with Fran; and this had an interesting effect on their experiences. Where some of Fran's group members had been able enough to be trusties in the hospital, this second group had had much more negative experiences; their experiences had been more frightening, they had had even less control in these bleak places. There was no pleasure or satisfaction to be gained from recounting such events.

Some time later, a new, small day-centre for people with learning difficulties was opened, with Fran Seeley as head. We ran an eight session life-review group to help develop group cohesion. By 'life-review' I mean that at the beginning of each session, we suggested an age-span we thought the group might like to focus on. We also constructed diagrams with them of whom they lived with when young, and who they lived with now. What was obvious was their happiness when young before being stigmatized. This group was extensively researched (Bender and Tombs 1992) and showed levels of engagement and therapeutic activity very similar to a psychotherapy group I was running for cognitively competent older people. Our research also showed the effect of too wide a range of verbal ability – the less able hardly spoke. In this case this was inevitable as we wanted to include all centre users; but again it pointed to selecting people of similar verbal ability, so that the pace suits most, if not all, of the group members. But this range of verbal ability did not hinder conversations *outside* the group, nor the development of strong group cohesion. This cohesion was put to positive use. When the reminiscence group finished, the 'slot' was used for a house committee of all the day-centre users. This group, six months on, runs itself, takes its own decisions and minutes; and the chairperson was initially one of the quietest and shyest members.

This example of what can be achieved by giving a group of devalued people a surrounding structure of respect and a belief in their potential shows what ability and experience lies untapped. It's there if we quietly provide the right conditions.

Reminiscence groupwork with people who have severe dementia

I never really knew what 'severe dementia' was when I worked for Social Services. This was because the term is usually used in a comparative sense, to refer to the most confused residents in the unit, who in fact may not be very confused at all. Once I started working in the continuing care (i.e. long-stay) wards, this point was all too forcefully apparent. For example, with some patients, the use of 'smells' kits in bottles is quite inappropriate as they will try to eat the bottles. But these difficulties should not deter us from attempting to modify our methods to make them applicable to these units. The sessions last only thirty or forty minutes and use physical objects (e.g. gas masks, clothes, etc.) and auditory stimuli. Our research data show a member: staff ratio of 2:1 is needed, compared to the more usual 3:1 or 4:1 for more cognitively competent groups. Such groups are very exhausting, as group leaders need to be attentive at all times so as to pick up and encourage the least response.

A level of engagement (paying attention) can be achieved 70 per cent of the time once the group has met for a few sessions. This contrasts to an engagement level of about 20 per cent for the same members at the same time of day when on the ward and not taking part in any activity (McKiernan and Yardley 1991). *But* note most of this effect is due to providing an activity that is relevant or of interest to the members of a group with committed group leaders. Thus, a group focusing on sensory stimulation, with similar clients on the same wards, produced similar levels of engagement (Mowle-Clarke *et al.* 1992).

I would estimate that about a third of patients on such continuing care units can gain some benefit and satisfaction from reminiscence groups. Obviously, this will vary greatly between units, because the severity of attention and memory loss will also vary considerably.

The supervision of the leaders of such groups should be very regular and provide active structure and support. A key aspect of the supervisor's role is to share the joy and triumph of small improvements.

A slow-beating drum: working with people who have become dependent on the psychiatric system

Groups move at different paces and group leaders must respect this and go at the pace of the group, even when this is not the pace of other groups they've led or at the pace they would like to move at. This is very apparent in a group I've been supervising composed of older (fifty plus) women who have been in the psychiatric system for many years and now attend a day hospital. This group, whose membership has changed little, meets for eight sessions, then breaks for four weeks or so, and is reconstituted. At the beginning, the members were quite unused to being in a group that talked personally. Gradually, their conversation became more personal; but the rate of change is far slower than most groups I have run, e.g. groups whose members have a learning difficulty, who usually relish the opportunity to explore their lives. So the task of the supervisor is to allow the group leaders to enjoy their small gains to the full; and stop wanting to shake the members into faster movement.

One feature of working in day hospitals is that frequently group leaders have a serious conflict of roles. In the group, they are democratic, treating the group members as equals capable of autonomous action, and they communicate their wish that the members should feel able to raise personal issues in the group. Outside the group, however, they may well be the key worker of one or more of the members, with a powerful one-to-one relationship. They may be giving the member depot (long-lasting) injections; in short, giving a quite different set of messages.

The same set of role conflicts can, of course, occur in other settings where the worker has management responsibility for the client. But it appears sharpest in nursing settings; with staff shortages, it is often impossible to separate the roles. I have felt it better to live with this conflict and look at the conflicts as they arise in the sessions, being aware that they are not always resolvable, rather than have no groups.

After the second block, I interviewed the potential members for each new block of eight sessions with the group leaders. (Many of the members had been in previous blocks.) In this way, the supervisor is not some shadowy figure, and we ask for and gain 'informed consent' for the themes for the next block. Particularly gratifying as we now start the fifth block is that the members themselves want to explore their lives further, even, in one case, defying parental instructions not to talk personally. It's taken two years to get to this point.

With regard to 'informed consent', I am now much clearer that each would-be member, *whatever their level of cognitive competence*, must be interviewed individually by the team so that they know what they are agreeing to; again this should apply to all groups, be it bingo or psychotherapy. And in the first session (and longer if needed), the group needs to work out the rules it wants to abide by. A key area to be discussed is confidentiality. If people gossip about what is said in a group outside it, nothing of significance will be said. Alternatively, if confidentiality is a non-negotiable necessity, the group leaders could inform the members of this expectation *before* the group begins; and all the other rules can be worked out by the group as it develops.

Another use of reminiscence groups is to encourage members to re-establish relationships outside the group. For example, the task for a given set of sessions can be for each member to build up their family tree (Burnham 1986). Besides generating personal information and experiences common to the group members, in order to gain the information needed, the members need to make contact with relatives and friends. Such contacts may have withered or been broken, but now they have a reason to re-establish them. Certainly, Kay Isbell, who was a community worker with old people brought up on the Barbican, found this a powerful way of helping people re-form their networks.

Across the generations

The respect in which the older members of a society are held by the younger members is a function of the rate of technological change – at what rate is their knowledge becoming obsolescent? But there are opportunities for continuities of culture over and above technology.

So we can utilize reminiscence in two ways. First, to help older people explore the meaning of their lives, in which case accuracy of memory is less important. Second, however, older people are also capable of providing valuable oral history (Thompson 1988; Bender 1991b), which can be checked for accuracy against written records.

Paulette Bauckham and I arranged for residents in local authority homes to give talks to secondary school children at the local school, which were very well received both by the children and their teachers. Also, after running two groups in the local museum in Kingsbridge (Bender 1992), we made links between the day-centre and the primary school, whose children, in small groups, interviewed members on various aspects of their lives; they presented copies of their illustrated essays to the day-centre. We hope clients will give a number of short lessons on various aspects of their lives in the school. In this way, we can get across to the children the role of older people as valuable custodians of their (the children's) cultural heritage.

We can also use the old person's geographical identity as a starting point for their self-exploration. So, membership of a group entitled 'A walk down Fore Street' (Kingsbridge's main street) is open to all clients who have lived in the town for 25 years. They can explore their relationship with the town and their lives in it in any way they choose – historical research, painting, autobiography, poetry, writing. Whatever they wish, we try to provide the resources.

In these ways, then, the role of the older person as 'oral historian' can be used to develop new roles, new links and enrich their lives.

The relationship of reminiscence groupwork to therapy

Buchanan and Middleton (this volume) pose a challenging paradox, that proponents of reminiscence are suggesting that it is a technique that is readily useable by untrained staff, but also that it has therapeutic features which raise it above entertainment or stimulation and therefore, such work needs lengthy professional training. Can these claims, which have undoubtedly been made, be resolved? I have thought about this question many times, when working with talented but untrained staff, and it seems to me the answer – or at least part of it – lies in the different answers to two questions: is reminiscence groupwork (a type of) therapy and can reminiscence groupwork be therapeutic? Let us take each question in turn:

Is reminiscence groupwork therapy?

The answer is clearly 'No'. Therapy, as commonly understood, occurs (1) when a person, commonly called the patient, (2) perceives at some level that they have a problem and (3) is referred or, less commonly, refers themselves to a mental health specialist. (4) After an assessment, (5) the specialist and patient agree on a formulation of the patient's problems. (6) The therapist, selecting from a number of possible approaches or techniques – although I am aware that sadly many therapists offer treatment from only one school of therapy – (7) offers the most suitable one to the patient, who (8) consents.

We can see that the usual reminiscence group fulfils none of these criteria. Most centrally, the member does not come believing he or she has a number of problems that the therapist will help them tackle. So, *does this mean reminiscence groupwork has no benefit?* Because reminiscence work is not therapy, this in no way implies that it is without benefit. Unfortunately, 'therapy' occupies the high ground of prestige, casting into shadow such usages as giving residents stimulation or activity; giving them one enjoyable hour a week to look forward to; building up cohesion in the group so that it can move into other purposes; rehabilitating communication and social skills, etc. All these are perfectly valid and extremely useful ends to which reminiscence can be directed. The concept of the Maslowian hierarchy of needs (Maslow 1970; Bender *et al.* 1990) is useful here. Basic needs have to be satisfied first. And until these needs are addressed, offering therapy is misguided. All that glitters in reminiscence work is not therapy; and we should not be tempted to distort perfectly valid uses of reminiscence work by either apologizing for them or pretending they are 'in fact' therapy.

So answering the first question is relatively simple and can be done by referring to a kind of 'trades description' definition. It is the answer to the second question that is rather more illuminating, and I will try and answer it through my own experience in groupwork.

Can reminiscence groupwork be therapeutic?

When Val Levens and I started running reminiscence groups for people with learning difficulties, we had no intention of running therapy groups. Yet, we noted the expression of strong emotions, high rates of self-disclosure and the sharing of painful experiences. So we seemed to be doing therapy without wanting to!

As I've said, we were *not* doing therapy, since the members had not presented themselves to the group with problems they wished to address. But we can improve this analysis further. Bloch and Crouch (1985) and Yalom (1985) have reviewed what experienced group therapists think makes for effective therapy. They found a high level of agreement between various

Table 3.1   Brief description of the eleven therapeutic factors

1   *Catharsis*: expressing strong emotions about an event or situation and appearing more relaxed afterwards.
2   *Self-disclosure*: revealing personal information not previously communicated to the group.
3   *Relating more openly*: experimenting with more open ways of expressing feelings and relating to others.
4   *Universality*: realising that other members have had similar experiences and/or similar problems.
5   *Acceptance*: feeling accepted by the group and secure within it.
6   *Altruism*: member-to-member aid or the offer thereof.
7   *Guidance*: advice or information given by a leader to a member or members.
8   *Self-understanding*: member indicates evidence of new insight into self *and/or* their relationship to others.
9   *Vicarious learning*: learning through observation of other members' views or behaviour and strategies.
10   *Installation of hope*: optimism expressed as to progress within the groups or in life more generally.
11   *Agency*: member expresses 'ownership' or responsibility for present or past behaviour (exclude depressive self-blame).

writers as to what are the key *therapeutic* factors. There are usually about ten. However, Attribution Theory suggests that a key variable as to whether a person is coping with the demands of their environment is their belief that their behaviour can change what happens; that what they do matters. This belief is called 'agency' and seemed particularly important in making sense of the experience of people with a learning difficulty. I therefore added it to the ten proposed by Bloch and Crouch (1985) (see Table 3.1).

What happened in those groups was that I had been looking the wrong way. I thought that if we knew that these were *not* therapy groups, then they could not look or feel like them. But what had happened was that we had created a setting, a structure in which the members felt safe and secure and felt able to manifest these factors – self-disclosure, acceptance, catharsis, etc. Therapeutic effects were taking place.

A factor in my mistake may have been the assertion by the psychodynamic schools that insight is the key, the *sine qua non* of effective therapy. How could people with a learning difficulty show insight? But the research summarized by Bloch and Crouch (1985) suggested that insight was a relatively unimportant variable in getting better.

So, groups can have unintended therapeutic effects. What are the implications of this? It is useful to distinguish between *focused* and *identity* problems. Focused problems include such difficulties as phobias, bereavements and crises. Most people will have focused emotional problems at some time in their lives.

The only time I have used reminiscence for focused therapy was when I was asked by a psychiatric day hospital to help patients with blocked grief reactions concerning dead spouses. Since I do not feel at ease with confrontational techniques such as 'the empty chair', I decided to run a reminiscence group focusing on the themes of courtship and marriage. Obviously, this would involve the members talking about their dead spouses and I hoped thereby to help them detraumatize. The group was very successful. By the end of the ten sessions, the members were talking freely about the dying and deaths of their spouses, and even the arrangements they had made regarding their own funerals. Their new-found freedom was pleasing to observe. This is the only group I have run which fits the traditional definition of therapy (assess, define problem, design treatment programme to remove problem).

Identity problems

Let us now consider problems relating to a person's identity. All the client groups I am involved with have long-term problems. The people attending the psychiatric day hospital have had problems of dependency for years. Unable to find uncomplicated love from their parents and, as a result, failing to do so again in their marriages, they are seeking it from the workers in the psychiatric services. What they get isn't a satisfying substitute but it's the best they can get; and they have been stuck in these unsatisfactory relationships for years. It is for this reason that to aim to 'cure and discharge' such patients is completely misguided, since for them to go along with such aims would be to lose what little love they have. People with learning difficulties have a different set of long-term problems. They have never been allowed to choose; all their important life-choices are made for them, either by parents or by staff. Finally, 'the elderly'. This is a ludicrous phrase as it suggests that everyone over sixty-five has problems. In fact, the services deal with a small percentage of this age group. But people over sixty-five *do* have one common long-term problem. They suffer from a whole series of negative stereotypes, arising from their leaving the workplace – unproductive, their useful lives over, decrepit, senile, etc. Sadly, many, if not most, older people internalize these stereotypes and so come to believe them.

So all three groups have long-term problems, different for each client group, but sharing the long-term damage to their identity. We can see a therapeutic intent in helping them repair these damaged identities. I now want to explore the use of reminiscence in helping build or rebuild damaged identities. But, before doing so, I want to stress that people with long-term problems can also have focused problems but are often denied access to the mental health services which deal with them. For example, psychotherapy is very rarely offered to people with learning difficulties (Reiss *et al.* 1982; Hurley 1989) or to people over sixty (Hildebrand 1986). This injustice is a separate issue which will not be resolved by developing reminiscence work concerned with identity damage.

I believe that reminiscence groupwork could be of use in repairing identity damage, by helping the members see that their lives have a form and shape, by giving them a historical and geographical identity; occasionally, they would 're-work' puzzling parts of their lives so that the bits fit better. Most importantly, they would feel – perhaps for the first time – that they were being listened to and their experiences respected by high-status persons. Such a change would take time, requiring many sessions.

Having spelt out a possible programme and rationale of therapeutic reminiscence groupwork, we can now return to Buchanan and Middleton's challenge.

Can reminiscence groups be run by untrained staff?

The answer is 'Yes' *if* they are supervised by a person who has experience of groupwork and a clear theoretical grasp of the group's function. It is this combination – staff with the ability to relate and respect and competent supervision – that is required for effective groupwork.

There are other conditions that relate to the environment in which the group takes place. I will therefore try to spell out some of the major determinants of successful reminiscence groupwork.

1 Suitable staff: the group leader must like the members of the group, and be able to clearly communicate respect and interest in what they are saying. They require one further attribute: they must be open to supervision and the changes it implies in the way they behave towards others. Some people do not have this openness – any comment immediately ruffles their feathers.
2 A competent supervisor who understands what happens in groups and how they develop; and how what is happening relates to the goals of the group. If you like, they work the rudder.
3 Sufficient time for supervision: this is a more difficult achievement. While officers in charge of units may clear their staff to run a group, they may have great difficulty understanding the need for supervision, since the welfare and health systems are so bad at caring for their staff's emotional health.
4 The purpose of such groups needs to be fully explained to possible members in an individual session and informed consent gained.
5 I do not think that all people with a damaged identity would wish to join such a group. There would be limits to any benefit set by very severe cognitive disabilities. Also, many will see no purpose in examining their identity – they have come to terms with societal devaluation and don't wish to disturb their defences (Sinason 1992).
6 The surrounding environment should allow members to develop their new identities. Groupwork is a delicate flower. It can produce major changes but these are very susceptible to being crushed and ground underfoot if the environment within which it takes place is uncaring or actively hostile; or, more exactly, threatened by the development of its clients' personalities. The group workers and their supervisor have a responsibility to ensure that the 'receiving' environments will at least be neutral to changes in their clients as a result of the group. If they are negative, the group should not be started and the efforts of the group workers should be spent trying to change the destructiveness of these environments.

So, there are a number of quite major conditions for this reminiscence groupwork to be successful, and the psychologist, or any other mental health worker, who sells reminiscence as an activity anyone can do without training or awareness of the issues involved, is acting unprofessionally, especially since they are betraying clients they are pretending to help, by failing to specify the conditions essential for effective groupwork and then, to the best of their ability, seeking to achieve them.

Looking forward, looking back

There is one more confusion that needs to be highlighted and which I wish to end on. On the one hand, reminiscence can be used for a fun group, but it can also be used to help people explore very painful aspects of their lives; after all, much of the history-taking in initial therapy interviews is effectively structured reminiscence. Therefore, done clumsily and without an understanding of what they are doing, reminiscence workers can cause considerable and unnecessary pain. Or to put it another way, reminiscence is a powerful technique and therefore it can be used well or badly.

With this point in mind – it's a point that has been both recognized and ignored in psychotherapy for some years – it becomes essential that we know why we're running groups, i.e. what is their purpose? Since reminiscence is a technique, it follows that it must be used for an end. No group should be called simply 'a reminiscence group'. One clear sign of a good group leader is clarity of purpose, knowing why they are running the group. If they don't know that, they can't know what's relevant and what's irrelevant to their goal. A clear purpose keeps them and the group on track. So, a group aimed at stimulating residents has stimulation as its goal. Once that is understood, we can ask: How else besides reminiscence can we stimulate these residents? Add some keep-fit? A news quiz? A bit of reality orientation as to events coming up?

So, reminiscence must always be a means to an end. It must always serve a master other than itself; and towards the end of any group, we must return ourselves and our members to the present, so that they can continue what they have gained in the group. This is the case whether we have used reminiscence for enjoyment or for some other end. If the members enjoyed being stimulated by talking about the past, how can their discussions continue if no staff are available – by themselves in one of the smaller lounges? If they made friends in the group, how can these friendship perhaps be continued? If one of them sees their relationship with their brother differently now, can that different perspective be brought to bear to improve their relationship with him? There are infinite possibilities.

It isn't always possible to achieve therapeutic changes because of a negative environment. So you may have (and I have had) the unenviable choice of trying to work in such negative environments or walking away. I found this particularly depressing when the situation concerned people with a learning difficulty.

On the plus side, there is that lovely moment, a few sessions into the life of a group, when you notice that you're not saying much and that you feel relaxed and you know that the group no longer needs you as the provider of energy. They can now sort out their own problems, they can set their own agenda. To add to the wealth of experience that is their lives, they now have confidence and trust.

The wisdom is in the group.

Acknowledgements

I should like to thank Ron Wood and Charles Goodson for their supervision, Alison Bender for her comments on the manuscript and Lynne Barnes for typing the chapter in its various drafts.

4

What can reminiscence contribute to people with dementia?

FAITH GIBSON

There is widespread interest in using reminiscence as a means of enhancing the quality of life of older people and some practitioners have transferred what is generally known about reminiscence to their work with people with dementia. This chapter seeks to explore the relevance of reminiscence to people with dementia and suggests that there needs to be very careful critical scrutiny, modification and adaptation of general reminiscence work if its inherently rich potential is to be used effectively with people with dementia.

Although there is continuing debate about the nature, prevalence, incidence and natural course of the different conditions described by the term dementia, it is widely agreed that whether dementia is conceptualized according to perspectives from clinical medicine, psychology or sociology, people so described are vulnerable to social isolation, estrangement and loneliness. They tend to be experienced as an increasing burden to themselves and to those who live and work with them as either family or professional carers. The clinical medical view stresses that dementia refers to a group of degenerative organic diseases of the brain which impair memory, thinking and behaviour. They are irreversible, progressive and terminal. Alzheimer's disease is the most well known and often this term is used loosely to refer to all dementias, regardless of type. Kitwood (1989, 1990, 1992) has suggested that a dynamic interplay between neurological and social–psychological factors offers a less deterministic, more comprehensive explanation of these disorders and argues that this view fits better with the experience of people who care for others with dementia.

Whichever viewpoint is held, people with dementia become increasingly disengaged and prone to behave in ways which lessen their opportunities for social interaction. In the early stages of dementia, people may feel acutely anxious and increasingly depressed (Froggatt 1988) as they become aware of failing memory and its associated problems.

Dementia commonly shows itself in increasing impairment of capacity for mastering new learning, disturbance of language skills, increasing difficulty in recalling the past and retrieval of old learning, although memory for more distant times and places, events and people may appear relatively unimpaired compared with the ability to remember the recent past. Often dementia leads to disorientation in time and place, changes in mood, personality and behaviour, loss of social skills, restlessness, agitation, unawareness of danger, progressive loss of motor control, often including incontinence and the capacity for self-care. The age of onset, severity and speed of deterioration in cognitive and physical capacities varies greatly and incidence increases with age (Jorm and Korten 1988).

Any intervention which seeks either to halt such deterioration or offer any means of constructive help is likely to be seized upon with great enthusiasm. Faced with the threat to personhood inherent in such multiple changes brought about by diminishing cognitive functioning, the attendant be- havioural difficulties, the loss of personal control, encroaching solitariness, the burdens and distress of family carers and the prevailing pessimism of most professional carers, the question 'what can reminiscence contribute to people with dementia?' is extremely important. Along with the timely reappraisal of reality orientation (Woods *et al.* 1992), the increasing emphasis on social stimulation and activity (Jones and Miesen 1992) and the attention being paid to validation therapy (Feil 1982, 1992), reminiscence is growing in popularity (Bornat 1989). The ideas presented in this chapter arise from the writer's wide experience of reminiscence work and draw particularly on two very different practice-based projects. The first, undertaken in 1986, applied general ideas about group reminiscence (Help the Aged 1981; Gibson 1984). This project established and evaluated 25 short life reminiscence groups in residential homes and day-centres. The majority of participants did not have memory problems but a small number did and had been assessed as having dementia. Reflection on the undoubted success of this groupwork for people without dementia and the relatively limited efficacy of this general approach for the group members with dementia, led to the development of a taxonomy which distinguishes between 'general' and 'specific' reminiscence work undertaken with people with dementia and with people with no dementia and between groupwork and individual work. These distinctions are illustrated in Figures 4.1 and 4.2. A second project was subsequently developed to test ideas about 'specific' work with a small number of individuals with moderate to severe dementia. The first project could be said to be located in quadrant B in Figures 4.1 and 4.2 and the second project in quadrant C in Figure 4.1. The term 'general' reminiscence work refers to well-prepared work that uses a variety of multisensory triggers to stimulate shared conversation on an agreed topic or theme which relates loosely to the known background and interests of the participants. 'Specific' reminiscence work refers to carefully selected, highly focused, concentrated consistent efforts to stimulate recall and conversation using carefully selected triggers known to closely approximate the detailed life-history of the participant. Both approaches may be used in small groups or with individuals but 'specific' work is more easily managed with individuals.

Claims and counter-claims about the effectiveness of general reminiscence will not be rehearsed here. Because reminiscence refers to such a rich variety of different approaches, its evaluation also needs to use a variety of different

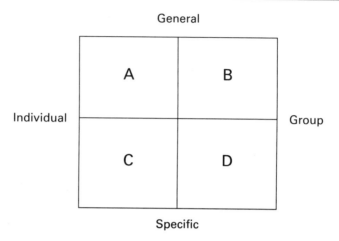

Figure 4.1 Reminiscence with people with dementia.

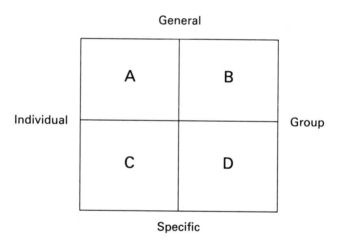

Figure 4.2 Reminiscence with people without dementia.

methodologies that take account of the defined objectives of any piece of work and the type of subjects involved. Few writers make such distinctions and most discuss reminiscence 'therapy' as if it were a uniform approach with universal applicability, whereas in practice it is a loose collection of disparate ideas resulting in varied activities undertaken with very different people in diverse circumstances. This lack of rigour leads to great confusion, to unsubstantiated claims about effectiveness and to a seemingly unbridgeable gulf between enthusiastic practitioners and critical researchers. Even the term 'reminiscence therapy' is misleading and 'reminiscence work' is preferable. 'Therapy' implies illness and systematic treatment by professionals who, if clever enough, will be able to effect a cure. 'Work' implies mutuality, shared experience and stresses positive rather than negative aspects of behaviour. It emphasizes and seeks to use a person's capacities that may still be intact, not those which are lost, what is healthy rather than diseased and to provide opportunities to exercise abilities, interests and capacities which still exist. This approach demands that carers recognize the personhood (Kitwood 1992) of the people they reminisce with and in this sense reminiscence may be truly therapeutic. Thus the reminiscence work undertaken in the two projects described, whether it was with individuals or groups, general or specific, undertaken with people who had dementia or with those who did not, sought to use the past in order to sensitively, creatively and imaginatively make it work for people in the present.

'General' group reminiscence

The first project aimed to evaluate the effectiveness of group reminiscence as a way of achieving change in old people and staff in four residential and two day-care facilities within a statutory social services department. Its objectives were to establish reminiscence groups of limited duration with agreed membership consisting of older people and staff who would meet together with a project worker to engage in reminiscence work using a variety of trigger materials and programmes.

The project team consisted of the writer and two graduate assistants who undertook the formation of groups and acted as co-leaders together with staff members. Each project assistant was attached to two residential homes and a day-centre throughout the project. Staff were selected by the facility managers and briefed by the project assistants. Senior staff suggested potential group members but over the lifetime of the project it was hoped that all residents or day-centre members would have an opportunity to participate if they wished to do so. Freedom of choice about participation was strongly emphasized by the project team, bearing in mind that reminiscence does not suit everyone (Coleman 1986). All possible members were interviewed informally by the project assistants in order to invite them to a group (which varied in size from six to ten members), explain its purpose and gather brief information about background interests so as to identify initial themes and relevant multisensory trigger materials. If the understanding of some of the potential members was limited, they were still afforded the same explanations and courtesies. A broad contract was agreed with members and staff about the number and time of sessions for each of the groups. At each session, the content of subsequent sessions was always agreed with the group. The exceptions to formed groups with closed membership were two homes where all the residents with dementia shared a common sitting room and here two large informal groups were attempted.

Twenty-five short-life small reminiscence groups involving 164 older people and 38 staff met for a total of 159 ninety-minute weekly sessions over a period of ten months. These were formed groups with a closed membership where a member was defined as someone who attended two or more sessions. One of the day-centres only had sufficient members to support two groups over four months and an additional informal group meeting on a drop-in basis. The groups engaged in reminiscence using a thematic approach and a variety of multisensory trigger materials, including slide packages such as *Do You Mind the*

Table 4.1   Participation showing total number of groups, sessions and membership

Facility	Groups	Total sessions	Members			Non-members	Staff	Volunteers
			Male	Female	Total			
Armour Day Centre	5	28	18	24	42	2	5	–
Coleraine Day Centre[1]	3	18	4	19	23	1	3	–
Brookgreen[2]	5	33	4	21	25	20	7	1
Metropole	3	23	6	16	22	2	4	1
Rathmoyle[3]	4	30	5	17	22	18	7	–
Roddens	5	27	10	20	30	3	12	–
Total	25	159	47	117	164	46	38	2

[1] Includes ten people attending an informal social centre, not strictly day-centre members.
[2] Includes as non-members ten people from informal lounge group.
[3] Includes as non-members eleven people from informal lounge group and six temporary holiday residents.

Time? Northern Ireland Recall (Gibson 1984). Membership and participation is summarized in Table 4.1. Of the total of 164 members, 47 were men and 117 women. Forty-six additional people were described as non-members because although they may have attended two or more sessions, they were either short-term respite care residents or else they belonged to the large informal groups using a common sitting area. The age and attendance records are summarized in Table 4.2. The wide age span was due to a small number of younger women with learning difficulties who liked to accompany their older friends to the reminiscence group. Both day-centres had a mixed clientele, but the smaller one set aside two days each week for people with moderate to severe dementia with the objectives of providing social and intellectual stimulation and carer relief. This was the only facility where reminiscence work was already established prior to the project. The staff preferred a more spontaneous approach to programming and found the project's requirement of a group meeting on a set day at a regular time somewhat constraining. Nevertheless, they gladly cooperated and the officer-in-charge as well as other staff participated. Some of the seventeen residential homes' groups contained no members with dementia, some had a mixed membership and a small number were exclusively for people with dementia.

The project assistants made detailed written records of each group session and many were also tape-recorded. I subsequently analysed the extensive records in terms of programme, attendance, interactions, emotional climate and content of the reminiscences. I also undertook semi-structured interviews with the officers in charge of the facilities and their line managers to ascertain their views about the effectiveness of the project for the group members and staff. The project assistants collated the views on satisfaction and effectiveness of participating staff and members shortly after the final session of each group. When views were solicited from a number of sources, namely participants,

Table 4.2 Characteristics of members by age: Attendance of members and staff

Facility	Age range (years)	Median age (years)	% Members with no absences	% Members not more than 2 absences	% Sessions attended by 1 staff member
Armour Day Centre	43–84	68	43	64	71
Coleraine Day Centre	50–91	71	17	48	85
Brookgreen	63–93	85	68	92	67
Metropole	62–99	73	82	95	96
Rathmoyle	63–96	80	50	55	40
Roddens	69–97	81	50	67	78

staff, senior staff and managers, and were supplemented by an analysis of the project assistants' records, a picture emerged which makes it possible to advance ideas about good practice in general reminiscence groupwork.

The detailed outcomes of this project for the participants who did not have dementia have been reported elsewhere (Gibson 1987, 1989a). Here only the outcomes for the members with dementia are addressed. In all the mixed membership groups studied, where some people had dementia and others did not, it was found that the people with dementia showed substantial evidence of pleasure and enjoyment. They appeared to be delighted with their experience of recall, even if their recollections were seemingly soon forgotten. In these groups, the impaired members joined in without difficulty and appeared little different in the group context from the others who were always tolerant and encouraging. The project assistants reported that within the mixed groups, aberrant behaviour, although commonplace in the general life of the residential homes, was rarely displayed. The project assistants modelled warm accepting behaviour which reinforced relevant contributions made to the discussion by all the members, and both the project assistants and staff volunteered that members with dementia 'passed' themselves very successfully in these mixed groups. They were able to participate with pleasure to themselves and without disruption or distraction to the other members.

Staff reported that for some of the people with dementia throughout the weeks they were participating in the groups, marked restlessness and agitation was reduced, appetite improved and almost all the members appeared to enjoy the change in institutional routines when, at the time the project was running, alternative small group activities were virtually non-existent. It was unfortunately not possible to determine whether such gains persisted over time.

A similar picture emerged in the mixed day-centre groups. The reported outcomes for the group in the small day-centre consisting entirely of people with dementia were scrutinized closely. Here it was apparent that almost all the communication took place between either staff or project worker and members. Rarely was there conversation between members as happened in the mixed membership groups. Some individuals derived great satisfaction from their conversation with staff, as illustrated by one habitually silent man who, when viewing slides of rural life, responded with animation. When shown a picture of a blacksmith's forge, he correctly identified and named a one-time local blacksmith. His unexpected achievement, corroborated by his sister with whom he lived, greatly encouraged the staff in persevering in their hitherto unsuccessful efforts to communicate with him. Many but not all staff demonstrated an increased understanding of individual group members and said they were surprised that people whom they thought they knew well and whom they believed to be seriously impaired could so actively participate in reminiscence groups.

A marked contrast to the limited achievements within these small intimate groups was the experience within the two large unformed groups of 11–13 people with dementia who happened to share a common sitting area. Here two or possibly three individuals may have derived some minor transitory pleasure from their one-to-one encounters with the project worker, like smiling when handed an artefact, drawing a hand away from a flat iron as if expecting it to be hot, or tapping a foot almost imperceptibly in response to music but very little else was achieved. One participant's behaviour markedly deteriorated and staff blamed the reminiscence group for her increased aggression and agitation.

By reflecting on the experience in different kinds of groups in terms of size, membership, staff involvement, location and programme, and comparing the outcomes of the formed and unformed groups, much was learned about general reminiscence groupwork with people with dementia. We concluded that the reminiscence work undertaken had yielded some relatively minor gains for people with dementia and their staff carers and went on to formulate the following guidelines:

1   Staff or volunteers undertaking reminiscence work need training (Gibson 1989a). It is not sufficient simply to involve people in groupwork and expect them to learn from modelling or demonstration.
2   Workers need to set realistic explicit objectives and commit time to meticulous detailed planning.
3   Senior staff need to be fully committed to reminiscence work.
4   Simple honest explanations and invitations need to be extended. No-one should be dragooned.
5   Venues for group meetings need to insure freedom from intrusive distractions. With restless members it is best to leave the door ajar and not to prevent people leaving if they so wish.
6   Groups must be small, with no more than two to four carefully selected members. Each person needs to be attended to, encouraged to participate and their contribution valued.
7   Hyperactive or aggressive people are best excluded from groupwork, but they may well respond to individual work.
8   More than one leader or helper is desirable in order to give concentrated attention to individuals and to cope with behavioural problems. It is helpful if leaders share the same accent, idiom, ethnicity and outlook of group members.
9   Help reduce the risk of scapegoating by including more than one member of the same sex, disability or ethnic background.
10 People with hearing or visual difficulties may gain more from individual work, although many enjoy the company of a group. Communication

aids of various kinds and 'interpreters' or 'translators' sitting next to members with sensory difficulties can be helpful.

11 Frequent short sessions may be desirable. Length needs to be adjusted to suit the mood of the group. Different times of day may be better for different people.

12 Successful co-working requires effort. Group leaders may be staff members and they may be volunteers. It is essential that workers share respect for persons, are clear about mutual roles and responsibilities and are supported by senior managers.

13 The more closely the triggers used relate to the life-experience and interests of the members, the more evocative they will be. Multisensory triggers help compensate for different sensory and cognitive impairments. Artefacts which can be touched, handled and passed around as well as music seem to be particularly evocative.

14 Group meetings are enriched by serving tea, coffee or other beverages and once familiar food.

15 All reminiscence takes time and groupwork cannot be rushed.

16 Conversation should be set within safe territory and initiated by workers who need to respond to underlying emotional content rather than pursue factual accuracy.

17 Keep simple records of sessions and review these with someone else so as to reflect on ways of improving practice.

Even with very skilled work, the response achieved may be slight, almost imperceptible, but the small gains can be enormously important for the person with dementia and for their carers. The fact that pleasure may be fleeting or transitory does not negate its value either to the person or carer who often can be encouraged by such responses to persevere in their caring role.

'Special' individual reminiscence

The second project was very different in size, objectives and location. It developed from reflection on the earlier groupwork project and from further reading and practice. The earlier experience of group reminiscence had suggested that using reminiscence in highly focused, intensive and special ways with individual people with dementia may possibly be more fruitful than general groupwork. This second project involved a series of five case studies of four women and one man whose ages ranged from seventy to eighty-five years. In order to develop ideas about the practice of 'specific' reminiscence work with individuals with dementia (Fig. 4.1, quadrant C), I invited officers in charge of three statutory specialist homes for elderly mentally infirm people (known as EMI homes) to select their most 'troubled and troubling resident'. They were asked to commit staff time by attaching a senior care assistant as key worker to each identified individual in order to see whether or not it might be possible for this worker to use reminiscence as a means of ameliorating or modifying challenging or disturbing behaviour. Subsequently, a statutory specialist elderly care fieldwork team joined this second project to work in similar ways with two identified clients who lived in the community. The justification for this selective or 'creative justice' (Docker Drysdale 1968, 1973) approach is two-fold. First, the troubling individual is worthy of help in his or her own right. Individualization is now readily accepted as a major principle in child care practice but is still all too rare in gerontological care. Second, if the behaviour of the troubled and troubling people could be improved, then the quality of life for everyone else around them — residents, families and staff — could also be improved. By making things better for them, things could be improved for others. It was also thought that if 'specific' individual reminiscence work could make a difference to very difficult people, the lessons learnt might be more easily applied to others.

Evaluation rested on an analysis of written and verbal reports prepared by the key workers, officers in charge and line managers, and periodic meetings of all staff involved to ascertain their views about the project, which ran for ten months during 1990–91. It is readily acknowledged that this is a small number of case studies, yet this approach highlighted qualitative aspects of reminiscence work which others may wish to test. To provide a conceptual framework for this 'specific' individual work, eight stages of work were identified and each worker was free to proceed as best fitted their particular residential or community setting. The stages of work were as follows: achieving the backing of management; identifying the subject person; special observation; compiling a detailed life-history; planning the special work, including making a written care plan; implementing the plan; evaluating the work; and continuing the work and generalizing from it.

Everyone when asked to identify their most troubling resident could immediately do so. The people chosen varied greatly. Some were noisy, hostile, aggressive, disruptive, violent and non-conforming (Mary and Elizabeth). Some were very suspicious (Mary and Anabel) and two (Andy and Joan) were so withdrawn and silent that workers worried they paid them so little attention.

As in the earlier groupwork project, the backing of senior managers was paramount. Senior staff had to take responsibility for explaining to their staff the nature of this specialized focused work with identified individuals. Without this explicit support, the burden of departing from the established conventional routine ways of caring was too great for the key workers to carry, their work was too isolated, lacked reinforcement and could be sabotaged in innumerable ways by colleagues who were not committed to it.

An example of such subversion was in a home where the officer in charge had given little more than lip service to the project. The resident identified for 'specific' work was Mary, a very underweight, unhappy, isolated, hostile woman who spat, shouted, kicked or pushed anyone who came within reach. In the process of gathering her life-history, the key worker had found out from the woman's niece that Mary used to like 'nice things' such as fine china, good linen and flowers. So the key worker decided to tempt her to eat by setting a breakfast tray with a linen traycloth, special china and a posy of flowers. On the days when the key worker was absent, the special attention was withdrawn because the cook refused to set the tray, so opposed was she to one resident being singled out for individual attention.

The head of home was aware of the cook's attitude but avoided confronting her for several weeks because of her own ambivalence about the project. Eventually, encouraged by myself, she instructed the cook not to subvert the care plan and set the tray. Other staff also objected to this resident getting special attention and some remained sceptical to the end, despite acknowledging marked improvements in Mary's behaviour.

Two homes began with a period of very close observation. Simple proformas were used to record observations made by both key workers and other staff throughout the twenty-four hour cycle over several days in order to identify any patterns of recurring behaviour or times of the day or night when the person was particularly disturbed. Time spent alone, interactions with others, and preferences for where and how time was spent were all recorded. The here and now observations were very detailed and covered the following: social interaction with residents, staff and others; the relevance and appropriateness of behaviour; nature, content, coherence of speech and whether it was initiated or responsive; variations in lucidity, activity level and mood, especially around major events in the day like getting up, going to bed, bathing, toileting and meal times; personal preferences for food; preferred company; activities; ability to manage self-care; and contacts with family, friends, volunteers, staff and others.

In addition to drawing a detailed picture of the person's contemporary lifestyle, clues were elicited about significant past events, places and people. This led to the compilation of detailed life-histories which drew on all available sources of information including the older persons themselves and wherever possible their contemporary relatives and friends. Planned and spontaneous reminiscence with both the older person and his or her friends and family provided a major source of information about the life-histories which then suggested pointers to possible later work.

The person with dementia was a fruitful source of information and staff were encouraged to believe, rather than disbelieve, what was said. Often conversations needed to be decoded, but when staff began from the assumption of truth rather than falsity, belief rather than disbelief, worthwhile information was gleaned. Staff struggled to learn to decipher partial, symbolic and coded communications and to respond to people's underlying feelings rather than be preoccupied with establishing factual accuracy. This was very difficult because they were so accustomed to labelling people as 'confused' and, as a consequence dismissing seemingly incoherent conversation as confabulation, that they often failed to listen acutely and to empathize appropriately. This was especially true if the conversation was accompanied by tears or sadness when workers would either hastily change the conversation, try to distract or actually physically withdraw. When several bizarre stories were subsequently checked with relatives, they were found to be accurate in every detail. Because of their preconceptions, the workers had lost opportunities to gather past history and to explore past pain.

For example, Mary, who seldom talked other than to say 'Go to hell' to anyone who came near her, unexpectedly told the key worker she had once had a baby who had not lived long. Her records showed her as childless, so the worker did not respond. A relative later corroborated the story, saying Mary had had one child who died shortly after birth. The worker had missed an opportunity to empathize and relate to a painful experience which had leaked into the present, although it was a recollection of a loss which had occurred over fifty years before.

Another example was Andy, once a sociable, friendly man who had increasingly withdrawn into a private world and abandoned talking even to his devoted wife with whom he lived. During a planned reminiscence session held with him in a day-centre, he recounted a long tale about a family holiday at Niagara when a woman had thrown a baby over the Falls. Likewise, this was quickly dismissed but subsequently corroborated in minute detail by his wife.

The agency records almost always proved inadequate as others (Adams 1986; Meyers 1991) have found. They contained virtually no life-history information, being limited to assessments of contemporary functioning which was invariably reported in negative terms. The older people to whom these inadequate records referred were more like displaced persons, refugees, without a past, occupying the present but unconnected to it. Their whole long lives, the various roads by which they had travelled, their multiple intertwining biographies (Johnson 1978, 1988), had been reduced to a few short lines.

By actually reminiscing with the older people and their relatives, sometimes together, sometimes separately, comprehensive histories were gathered. Details of chronological events, family life and work, major life-crises, landmarks and transitions, places lived and visited, and personal idiosyncratic preferences were all important. Through reminiscing, the rich colour and fine-grained texture of a person's life was sketched. Some may think the information gathered was pedestrian. On the contrary, it provided the key to reaching into the increasingly private worlds now inhabited by these people.

Examples of questions asked included: where they were born and grew up; who was in their family; where they went to school; what had they, their parents and siblings worked at; where they spent their holidays; who were and are the important people in their lives; did they like fashionable clothes and jewellery; did they have their hair permed; did they use a hard or soft pillow or wake to an alarm clock; did they prefer sliced or unsliced bread; were they houseproud or casual; what were their hobbies and interests.

The reminiscence process itself, apart from yielding information which could be put to work for the person with dementia in the present, proved also to be valued by the older contemporary informants. Spouses especially said they were pleased to contribute to the care of their relatives in a world where they increasingly felt redundant, being able to do so little. On their own account, they were able to review (Butler 1963), rework and revalue the whole long life they had shared with the person who was inexorably becoming a solitary stranger.

All the key workers developed their own ideas about how they would use their newly acquired life-history knowledge. They were encouraged to make a written plan which could be modified at any time because creative work with people with dementia needs to be planned but flexible, responsive, spontaneous, free to proceed moment by moment within a broad overall framework. The plan was a guide to a possible journey, and if the journey took unexpected turns, then the worker would try to follow as best she could, being simultaneously finely tuned to present needs as well as to past history.

It does not matter if such written plans are called contracts (Schwartz 1971; Shulman 1979), goal plans (Barrowclough and Fleming 1986) or care plans (Holden and Woods 1988), provided they are ethical, relevant, responsive, flexible, practical, feasible, and specific about the behaviour expected of the key worker and the supporting roles to be played consistently by other staff or family carers. They must respect the person concerned and provide the maximum opportunity for them to be treated as unique valued individuals. The work proposed in the care plans was very varied. Even the additional attention at the observation and history-gathering stage was important because it signified heightened awareness of, and interest in, the older person and encouraged social interaction between them and others.

The detailed knowledge of the life-history was exploited in the present and used in many different ways. Trips, pilgrimages and activities which brought immense pleasure to the older person, key worker and others were undertaken. The reminiscence process provided the raw material for later work because it opened up conversational possibilities by giving clues and cues to potentially fruitful topics or themes. This seemed particularly important, because although the residential homes taking part in the project tried hard to provide an active care regime, day-to-day living could be experienced as monotonous, inward looking, boring, with little to distinguish one day from another and providing little stimulus to conversation. For example, Joan, a quiet withdrawn woman, her key worker and a member of the domestic staff with whom she had a good relationship went together to visit her sole surviving sibling who lived in a nursing home. Through reminiscing during the visit, Joan's lifelong love of greyhounds and dog racing came to light. She and the key worker had a night out at the dogs and the worker's enthusiastic report of a splendid outing was persuasively matched by a photograph of Joan laughingly patting the head of a winning dog.

The most obvious outcomes for the older people in the second project who received concentrated personal attention informed by detailed knowledge of their life-histories were undoubtedly increased sociability accompanied by decreased aggressive or seemingly attention-seeking behaviour. These changes were demonstrated in various minor ways. For example, an excerpt from Mary's key worker's records noted:

Hitherto she has always sat alone in the little lounge and would chase anyone who came near, using very colourful language. Mr. H, a new quiet resident was sitting in the room as well yesterday with two visitors. She let him sit on and thinking there would be trouble I suggested they should go to his bedroom. 'It's alright dear, let them stay' she said.

A later record noted:

Occasionally another resident will wander into her room. She doesn't shout at them now or hit out. She lets the domestic clean her room without fuss and actually talks to her, initiating conversation and calling her back to continue talking. She let three of us come into her room to admire her new dress and she seemed pleased to show it off.

On bad days she still sits looking at the floor, she will not come to the lounge. On good days she lifts her head and intermittently looks at people passing in the corridor. We have decided to turn her chair around so she can see people passing.

It was also possible to identify a number of consistent gains for staff. Both key workers and officers in charge said that reminiscence work of this highly individualized kind was a powerful and largely unexploited tool which had tremendous potential for staff development. Involvement in the project helped staff acknowledge their abysmal ignorance of the people in their care and the almost total lack of knowledge about the long and varied lives they had lived. Staff reported that compiling the life-history itself motivated both them and relatives. They became excited, intrigued and determined to discover and then to use the information they unearthed. Staff became fascinated with the person's past, and quickly grasped the possibility of using the life-history as a working tool to enrich the quality of social exchange in the present. They found they could put history to work. In recovering the past, the present came to life and the person with dementia shone through as a unique interesting individual. Sympathies were enlarged as the person was seen within the perspective of a whole long life and not just as they were in the present, demented, difficult and often demanding.

Staff learned to use detailed knowledge of the life-history to select triggers and to set up situations which related very closely to known interests and past activities so as to stimulate conversation and increase sociability. This deliberate use of tailor made triggers was particularly effective with Anabel who lived in a sheltered dwelling but who was thought to be at risk because of her encroaching dementia and increasing isolation. Meticulous research about the changing nature of her neighbourhood and detailed life-history gathering from a variety of sources were used to compile several reminiscence packs covering shopping and money, fashion and family events, and anniversaries. The packs consisted of old money, photographs, fashion catalogues, clothing and footwear. They were left in Anabel's house and used successfully by her daughters, home help, neighbourhood warden and community nurse to catch attention and focus conversation. When stimulated in this way, Anabel responded appropriately with a fair degree of accuracy and could sustain coherent conversation for several minutes. Both her daughters and the various paid carers felt better about their visits, her social isolation and its attendant risks were substantially reduced and she was able to continue to live at home.

A similar approach was used with Andy. He quickly deteriorated during the time of the project and became so impaired that he would dig the garden with a dust bin lid and put his feet down the lavatory but his wife was determined to care for him at home. A well-ordered family photograph collection matched with detailed recollections by his wife were used to initiate and sustain conversation. The worker found it imperative never to set Andy up for failure and always to locate the conversation within safe territory by taking the initiative to refer to known familiar places, people and events. Andy's after-lunch agitated restlessness was eliminated when his lifelong interest in classical guitar music was discovered while compiling his life-history. Although he could no longer play, he used to settle back in his favourite armchair and seemingly listen to guitar cassette recordings for up to an hour, thus decreasing the demands on his wife and prolonging her capacity for caring.

Other gains were identified. Staff preconceptions were challenged. Their habit of attaching labels, of engaging in self-fulfilling prophecy, was largely relinquished. They said that previously they had made assumptions on the flimsiest of evidence and there were many examples of staff getting the behaviour from residents which they had anticipated and sometimes helped to generate. The older person frequently conformed to the staff's expectations while real pain and loss went unrecognized, unregarded or unattended. For example, Elizabeth always disrupted mealtimes through constant shouting and messing with her food. Her life-history indicated that she had always found it hard to get up in the mornings, preferring to rise late. She was now encouraged to lie in, to take her time to get up, instead of being hassled by staff. For a time she was withdrawn from the dining room and ate only with her key worker, who paid her concentrated personal attention, frequently talking about past sporting interests. After several months she was able to return to the dining room to eat in company, without causing disruption.

The second project highlighted the advantages of trying wherever possible to keep people with dementia in known familiar surroundings. It suggested that if they have to move, it is worth trying to recreate as much familiarity as possible. Reminiscence work challenged institutional regimes. It heightened staff awareness and made it safe for them to question routines they had long taken for granted but which sometimes exacerbated rather than ameliorated disturbing and disturbed behaviour.

The intrinsic nature of reminiscence and life-history work demanded closer, more personal involvement between staff and older people, regardless of grade, status and training. Demarcation lines were blurred and staff no longer were satisfied just with providing good physical care within safe environments. They discovered that they could cope with difficult people, decrease their isolation and lessen their unhappiness. Instead of being told 'go to hell', they were told 'you care'. Instead of taking three staff to bath a person and cut her fingernails, they were asked 'would you give me a wash down please?' To see someone who habitually rejected most food ask for a second helping was rich reward indeed and job satisfaction was much increased.

Conclusion

The widely accepted social gains from general reminiscence work may now be taken for granted (Disch 1988). Reflecting on both projects reported here and on others' writings, especially McKiernan and Yardley (1991), Jones and Miesen (1992) and Kitwood (1992), it is possible to make tentative suggestions about the relevance of reminiscence work to people with dementia. If people have to move from familiar to unfamiliar surroundings, knowledge gained from a life-history compiled from all available sources, including reminiscence, can usefully guide the design, layout, furnishing, equipping, decorating and management of living environments.

General reminiscence in large groups using various multisensory triggers has limited diversionary and entertainment value. It is widely recognized that music is especially evocative. Social events such as tea dances, a night at the movies, mannequin parades, harvest suppers, outings and entertainments all have considerable reminiscence potential. To use reminiscence as a 'good old days' nostalgic entertainment is tempting to hard-pressed care staff. To do so, seriously limits its full possibilities for enriching the lives of older people. Such large group applications, as well as 'general' reminiscence in smaller formed groups, although of limited utility needs to be distinguished from planned focused 'special' reminiscence undertaken either with individuals or in very small groups.

There are many gains for carefully selected people with dementia, their families and professional carers from using well-planned, well-structured 'specific' reminiscence and life-history in highly focused ways in one-to-one situations. Reminiscence, either with people with dementia or not, does not suit everyone and so judicious selection is essential. People undertaking reminiscence work of whatever kind must seriously consider how best to convey a genuine free choice about participation.

The rich possibilities of deliberately using knowledge of a person's past to work for them in the present has scarcely begun to be exploited. The examples cited here point to some encouraging initial outcomes and justify further work. Reminiscence has a part to play in helping family carers sustain their caring and it has considerable potential as a staff development tool. By sensitively using knowledge of the past, it is possible to share to a much greater extent than is commonly thought possible, the encroaching private worlds inhabited by people with dementia. Such a view challenges prevailing professional pessimism and is by no means universally popular.

The search for islands of lucidity is demanding but fascinating work. Even if we fail to locate the intact parts of a person's memory, we may at least from their history glean an inkling of what it is they are trying to say. We may better understand the garbled story or jumbled sentence and be able to respond to underlying emotion. Such work means we must confront our own fears of feeling another's pain. We must to some extent at least be willing to enter into another's world and share another's experience. By doing this, we seek to join their time-scale rather than demand they join ours. In this way, we may accompany them on their journey, postponing the almost inevitable parting of the ways which usually comes as dementia progresses. Anything which delays or postpones that parting is worth trying and 'specific' reminiscence so far has proved a promising approach in sharing fleeting lucidity, transitory happiness and brief encounters.

5

Reminiscence reviewed:
A discourse analytic perspective

____ KEVIN BUCHANAN AND DAVID MIDDLETON _____

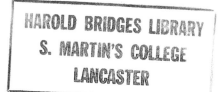

Introduction

Anecdote, evidence and variability

One striking feature of discussions of reminiscence work over the past ten years is a discrepancy between 'anecdotal' reports of the benefits of reminiscence for older people, produced by practitioners and proponents of reminiscence work, and the lack of any consistent 'hard evidence' of these benefits. This problem is referred to in all areas of the literature, from academic articles and conference papers (Merriam 1980; Thornton and Brotchie 1987; Bornat 1989; Norris 1989) through to training manuals (Gibson 1989a). Responses to this state of affairs have varied widely. On the one hand, some have taken this lack of evidence to signify that reminiscence has no special beneficial effects, and concluded that research into reminiscence should be abandoned (Thornton and Brotchie 1987) or refocused as part of a more general set of issues concerning the dynamics of small groups (Bender 1991a). On the other hand, others have argued that research has only just begun, and that rigorous empirical research will eventually corroborate anecdotal reports of benefits (Bornat 1989; Gibson 1989a).

In this chapter, rather than taking a position somewhere on this spectrum between optimism and pessimism, we will explore the problem from another perspective. We want to step back from discussion of the design or outcomes of research, and look instead at how the object of inquiry, 'reminiscence', is represented in the talk and writing of those involved in various ways with reminiscence work. We aim to show how an analysis of discourse about reminiscence can broaden our understanding of reminiscence work, and how it can throw new light on the 'evidence problem' referred to above.

Our concern, then, is with the variety of ways in which reminiscence is represented. This concern is not in itself something new to reminiscence research; most reviews of research over the last decade discuss variability in the definition and conceptualization of reminiscence. However, in these papers, variability is seen as an obstacle to the progress of research (Lo Gerfo 1980–81; Merriam 1980; Thornton and Brotchie 1987). The discourse analytic approach adopted here, rather than treating variability in the representation of reminiscence as a methodological problem, uses such variability as an analytical resource for research.

Discourse analysis

Our interest in variability reflects our interest in people's pragmatic use of language. Language, whether talk or text, is an active and constructive medium that people use resourcefully to accomplish things. One way of getting at what people are doing with language is to look at how its use varies according to the varieties of purposes talk and text can be taken as achieving. Potter and Wetherell (1987) have written a succinct introduction to this particular orientation towards the analysis of discourse. They point out that 'the constructive and flexible ways in which language is used should themselves become a central topic of study'.

To give an example, reminiscence work is sometimes represented as 'therapy', and at other times is explicitly represented as something other than therapy. Rather than seeking to decide between these two positions, on the basis of evidence and rational argument, we attend to what is being accomplished by these different representations; how they are used by speakers and authors to advance different kinds of arguments. More generally, debate about the 'therapeutic' status of reminiscence is just one way in which reminiscence is marked out and elaborated as an activity, irrespective of what conclusion you come to regarding its benefit to participants. Whether it is accorded the status of 'defence mechanism', 'oral history', 'pastime', 'therapy' or 'social movement', it is within the voicing of arguments for and against such representations that 'reminiscence' is constituted.

At the same time, these representations have implications beyond the immediate context of reminiscence work. For example, when people talk about the benefits of reminiscence for older people, this talk embodies assumptions about the nature of older people, and about what it is to be old. From the perspective taken here, such shared assumptions do not simply represent the 'reality' of old age; rather, they are the ways of representing old age that are culturally available to us. Just as there are different and contradictory ways of representing the nature and value of reminiscence, so too are there different and contradictory ways of representing the nature of ageing. Arguments about reminiscence work can be located as part of arguments about the nature of ageing and other broader cultural concerns which impinge on the practice of reminiscence work with older people. Our particular interest in this chapter is how representations of reminiscence are shaped by, and in turn contribute to, these broader cultural arguments.

Furthermore, in characterizing variability in representation as 'argument', we are marking the relevance of previous discourse analytic work which shows talk and thinking to have a rhetorical or argumentative structure (Billig 1987), and thus to embody contradictory or opposing views on its object (Billig *et al.*

1988; Middleton and Edwards 1990). One consequence of such work is that it directs us not merely to a consideration of variability, but to a consideration of contradictory representations of reminiscence and reminiscence work, as a means of identifying their functions and consequences in relation to broader social issues.

Reviewing reminiscence work from a discourse analytic perspective changes the focus of the research enterprise. Instead of studying reminiscence as an unambiguously definable activity or process which has determinate functions or effects, it is studied as something shaped by attempts to grapple with the problems and dilemmas inherent in reminiscence work. Variability in the way people represent reminiscence in writing and talk, be they practitioners, participants, policy makers or commentators, instead of being a problem to be solved or eradicated, becomes a major resource in understanding this constructive process.

In the following three sections, we examine a variety of representations of reminiscence, taken from the reminiscence literature, and from transcripts of interviews with those involved in reminiscence work. We aim to show how these various representations relate to contrary positions concerning three social practices impinging on reminiscence work: the social positioning of older people; the provision of care; and the exercise of therapeutic expertise. Following this, we discuss how the declared need for empirical evidence can be taken as deriving from the 'social argument' concerning the designation of reminiscence practice as 'therapy' and its consequent implication in moves to secure and define the expertise of psychologists. We end with some comments regarding the potential contribution of discourse analysis to the evaluation of reminiscence work.

Reminiscence and the social position of older people

Anyone familiar with reminiscence work will recognize the following ways of representing the value of reminiscence: reminiscence as oral history, perhaps as the fulfilment of a 'storytelling' role specific to older people; and reminiscence as protecting or enhancing the psychological well-being of the reminiscer. Many will also be familiar with the notion, often rehearsed in accounts of reminiscence work, that reminiscence was once seen as having no value, and was actively discouraged by carers of older people. However, the move to acknowledge that reminiscence *does* have value has taken a variety of forms. We will initially illustrate this in relation to various formulations of the 'social value' of reminiscence and then discuss their implications for the way authors formulate the social position of older people.

Contrary representations of the social value of reminiscence

The following two extracts typify contrary positions on the social value and consequences of reminiscence:

Extract 1
Although this mechanism may seem rigid and tiresome to other persons, this may be a way of maintaining self esteem. Therefore in studying the

aged and in caring for them, this pattern of reminiscing about identifying with one's past should be respected rather than treated as garrulous behaviour of no consequence.

(Lewis 1971:242)

Extract 2
Reminiscence preserves and transmits the cultural heritage and acknowledges that those who have lived history are its best teachers.

(Gibson 1989a: tape/slide notes 5)

Both these extracts mobilize arguments in favour of the value of reminiscence, but the way they do so has markedly different implications for what may be taken as its *social* value. Extract 1 is taken from a paper reporting the first experimental study of reminiscence by Lewis in 1971. In this paper, Lewis presents evidence that reminiscence may act as a psychological 'defence mechanism' in that, through identifying with their past accomplishments, older people avoid 'the discrepancy in self concept that old age represents to a formerly engaged and active member of society'. The argument in favour of reminiscence in Lewis's extract necessitates conditionally ascribing no *social* value to reminiscence ('may seem rigid and tiresome to others'; 'rather than treated as garrulous behaviour of no consequence'). This is then countered with the possibility of reminiscence having *personal* value as a way of 'maintaining self esteem'. By granting reminiscence as potentially 'rigid and tiresome' to others, its significance is represented and constructed as one that relates to the psychological well-being of older people as *individuals*, rather than as social agents.

This is in direct contrast to extract 2, taken from a reminiscence work training manual by Faith Gibson, published by Help the Aged in 1989. Here, social value is accorded to both the activity of reminiscence as a social practice, in that it 'preserves and transmits the cultural heritage', and to older people as agents in the transmission of cultural history – 'those who have lived history are its best teachers'.

Contrary representations of ageing and the social position of 'the elderly'

The two extracts, in ascribing different status to the social value of reminiscence, also embody contradictory representations of ageing, which have practical consequences for the social position granted to older people in society. Extract 1 can be seen as positioning older people as *marginal* to social life, in that reminiscence, what they have to say about their life-experience, has minimal value for others ('may seem rigid and tiresome to others'). Extract 2, however, clearly positions older people at the heart of social life.

These contrary ascriptions of *social position* to older people can be read as representing contrary views of ageing. For example, Lewis explicitly relates his view of reminiscence to 'disengagement theory' (Cumming and Henry 1961), which presents successful ageing as involving a process of withdrawal from social life, in preparation for the ultimate separation of death. Within such a view of ageing, the marginalization of older people appears to be both natural and appropriate. Such a theory formalizes a commonsense way of understanding ageing in our society, as a process of decrement and decline. Hockey and James (1990), for example, have argued that in 'western' cultures old age is understood in terms of *dependency*, and that one consequence of this is the social marginalization of older people. Gibson's extract, on the other hand, can be seen as embodying a view of ageing as the accumulation of experience and wisdom. This gives voice to a contrary commonsense view on the nature of ageing, according older people a special position in society as elders, and potential leaders, in virtue of their lived experience. Other authors have also noted ambiguities of response to old age (e.g. Slater 1964; Palmore 1971; Lowenthal 1985; Bury and Holme 1990).

These contrary representations of the consequences of ageing form part of an ongoing 'cultural argument' about the nature of ageing, and the consequent position of older people in society. The contrary representations of reminiscence we have identified embody opposing positions of this argument and, as 'lay notions' or 'scientific hypotheses', they derive their plausibility from these culturally available ways of understanding ageing and the place of older people in society. Moreover, these representations afford practical consequences for the social status of older people, in that they actively position older people as either marginally or centrally involved in social life. In construing reminiscence as a defence mechanism, we marginalize; in construing it as oral history, we 'demarginalize'.

Changes in the representation of reminiscence

The difference in time of publication between extracts 1 and 2 is some twenty years. Between those times, we can identify in the reminiscence literature a move from 'personal value' to 'social value' arguments and positions. Moreover, where the 'social value' position *is* taken in earlier texts, it is invoked in relation to other times or other cultures, rather than in relation to the time and culture of the author, as implied by extract 2. For example, McMahon and Rhudick (1964) discuss the social value of reminiscence in 'primitive' societies, where older people had an important role as 'storytellers'. Similarly, where the 'personal value' position is taken in later texts, it is invoked in relation to older people suffering from dementing illnesses, whose reminiscences are less likely to be considered socially valuable in cultural or community terms (e.g. Gibson 1989a:11). Furthermore, such reminiscences will often be represented as having social value in care settings, in so far as they 'personalize' relationships between staff and elderly clients (e.g. Norris and Abu El Eileh 1982), or provide valuable information about clients not obtained by formal assessment procedures (e.g. Norris 1989:28).

It is also common to find in the literature reference to the fact that reminiscence was once seen as a 'symptom' or 'cause' of mental deterioration, and was actively discouraged by carers of older people. Clearly, then, there has been a change over time in the relative prevalence of different representations of reminiscence. This change might be summarized as follows: once seen as having no value whatsoever, reminiscence came to be seen as having *personal* value, and then eventually as having *social* value.

One way of accounting for this change is to say that the 'true' value of reminiscence emerged over time; that reminiscence was once (mistakenly) seen as a 'symptom/cause' of mental deterioration, and that the 'natural' function of reminiscence, as a defence mechanism, or as the exercise of a social role, was discovered (or rediscovered) over this time through observation and research. We want to present an alternative account of this change, and argue that it embodies an active *repositioning* of older people in the discourse of ageing. The debate and discussion concerning the nature and efficacy of reminiscence maps a shift in the discourses of ageing, from one which potentially marginalizes older people to one which affords demarginalization. Moreover, the very *emergence* of reminiscence as an object of practice and research can be seen as a move in this repositioning process.

Reminiscence and repositioning 'the elderly'

To say that the rise of reminiscence is associated with a change in 'attitudes' to older people is not in itself new. For example, Coleman opens his definitive academic book on reminiscence with the statement: 'The last 25 years have seen an improvement in attention and respect paid to older people', and goes on to argue that 'a greater interest in older people's reminiscences . . . is also part of this development' (Coleman 1986:1).

Coleman's linking of reminiscence and 'attention and respect paid to older people' can be traced back to the first academic papers on reminiscence, produced in the 1960s and early 1970s. The way reminiscence is represented in these papers can be seen as beginning a process of repositioning older people in social terms, which has eventually culminated in the representation of reminiscence as having 'social value' as oral history. In the following discussion, we will focus on two of these papers, widely cited as seminal works in reminiscence research: Butler (1963) and Lewis (1971). Butler's paper is frequently referred to as *the* seminal work in the area; Lewis's paper is a report of the first experimental study of reminiscence.

These two authors present clinical and scientific evidence for the 'function-ality' of reminiscence in later life, as a 'life review mechanism' (Butler 1963:66) specific to old age, and as a 'defence mechanism' (Lewis 1971:243) against the vicissitudes of ageing. Both present reminiscence as a 'natural' process, occurring as part of another natural process, that of ageing. However, both then use this evidence to support a *moral* argument: that we should show more respect for the reminiscences of older people. In extract 1 above, Lewis ends his paper by arguing that reminiscing 'should be respected'. Butler makes a similar move in extract 3, encouraging us to 'listen . . . tolerate, and understand':

Extract 3
Recognition of the occurrence of such a vital process as the life review may help one to listen, to tolerate, and understand the aged, and not to treat reminiscence as devitalised and insignificant.

(Butler 1963:72)

Both authors are arguing against a view of older people's reminiscences as having no significance ('devitalised and insignificant', 'garrulous behaviour of no consequence'). However, they do *not* do this by arguing that reminiscence has value in terms of, say, the preservation and transmission of cultural heritage. On the contrary, they accept that it may have *no* apparent *social* value, but they argue that it may have *personal* value for the reminiscer, as 'a way of maintaining self esteem', or as a 'vital process', essential to the functioning of an ageing person. This assertion is then extended and used as a basis for arguing that reminiscence 'should be respected'.

In these two early papers, as well in other contemporaneous work (e.g. McMahon and Rhudick 1964; Lieberman and Falk 1971), reminiscence is 'naturalized'; talking about one's past experience is construed as a 'mechanism' or 'function' related to the 'natural process' of ageing. This 'naturalization' of reminiscence achieves two things. First, it opens the way for reminiscence to become an object of research and practice. Indeed, most accounts of the development of reminiscence work explicitly credit these papers (especially Butler's) with doing this. Second, this 'naturalization' can be seen as a constructive move in an argument for respecting older people. Representing reminiscence in this way entails a repositioning of older people socially. Constructing reminiscence as a functional necessity in a 'process' of ageing affords people the *right* to speak about their life-experience. Representing 'reminiscence' in this way means that it is no longer something which can be legitimately ignored or silenced. This repositioning process is taken further in the representation of reminiscence as oral history. From such a standpoint, older people do not only have the right to speak about their lives and experiences, but contribute special knowledge to others in doing so, and thus have a substantial part to play in the social life of any community.

Thus, we can see the 'personal value' representation of reminiscence, as presented in the writings of Butler and Lewis, as initiating a process of change in the discourse of ageing which has led eventually to the widespread espousement of the 'social value' position. This change in the way reminiscence is represented is not merely theoretical; it opens the way for changes in social practices, by providing arguments for the repositioning of older people in terms of their practical engagement with others. The very *emergence* of reminiscence as an object of practice and research, in the work of Butler and Lewis, can be seen as being implicated directly in a 'social argument' about the appropriate social position of older people.

Reminiscence and care: service and supervision

Reminiscence activities are very often provided as part of care programmes for older people, and reminiscence is claimed by many to have a transforming effect on the relationship between care workers and older people in receipt of care (e.g. Norris 1989; Bornat 1989; Gibson 1989a). In this section, we argue that there is a dilemma at the heart of the care relationship, and that this dilemma shows itself in contrary representations of the nature of reminiscence practice, as formulated in the discourse of those involved in reminiscence work.

The dilemma of care: service and supervision

The dilemma of care is that it is both serving and supervising. To take care of someone is to serve them by providing for their needs. At the same time, care involves management and supervision. To have someone 'in your charge' is to be 'in charge' of someone. In the process of providing for a person's needs, the provider assumes control, and this places the person provided for in a potentially dependent and subordinate position with regard to the provider. The dilemma is that, in the very act of giving, care provision potentially erodes autonomy and personal freedom.

Dissatisfaction with this authoritarian aspect of the care relationship has found voice in a variety of contexts, not least in relation to state provision for care of older people (e.g. Estes 1979; Phillipson 1989; Hockey and James 1990). In talk and writing about reminiscence, it is frequently presented as a means of democratizing care, and thus empowering its elderly recipients (see, for example, Langley and Kershaw 1982:16; Norris 1989; Thompson 1988:165). Extract 4, taken from a reminiscence training manual published by Help the Aged (Gibson 1989a), is a typical example of the representation of reminiscence as a democratizing, empowering activity:

Extract 4
Reminiscence work is often subversive and unsettling because it challenges conventional relationships between staff and older people, between
carers and cared for and it challenges management staff to revise and
reorder priorities. People, and listening to people may become more
important than maintaining present policies and prevailing regimes where
the first priority is physical care.

(Gibson 1989a:16)

Here, reminiscence is presented as anti-authoritarian – it is 'subversive and unsettling', it 'challenges management' practices, it may lead to the discontinuation of 'prevailing regimes'. It is an instrument of equality, by which relationships of differential status – 'carers and cared for', 'staff and older people' – may be recast as equal relations between 'people'. It is an instrument of democracy, in that, through 'listening to people', 'present policies and prevailing regimes' may no longer be maintained, may be discontinued or changed. The phrase 'listening to people' serves simultaneously as description of both reminiscence work, and the democratic process itself. Here, then, reminiscence is construed as a potential means of institutional change, a means of confronting the authoritarian structures by which 'carers and cared-for' alike are bound.

However, although reminiscence may challenge the conventional 'carer–cared for' relationship, it does not abolish it. Older people are still in the care of others, and the problematic of the care relationship remains. The provision of reminiscence as an aspect of care is construed as empowering, but the very act of provision can be seen as involving the exercise of authority. Thus, in the reminiscence literature, one can also find representations of reminiscence practice as *disempowering*, as in extract 5, taken from a recent conference paper:

Extract 5
It is perhaps inevitable, if regrettable, that reminiscence has occasionally
been left to become just another panacea or passing time activity in some
institutions. Now that its possible to buy boxes of photographs and
reminiscence stimuli, in some homes there is a fairly routinised approach
to reminiscence. The 'memories' group tends to take its place alongside
bingo and crafts.

(Bornat 1989:21)

Here, reminiscence is not democratizing or empowering; on the contrary, it is represented as potentially disempowering; as an activity which just 'passes' people's time, as part of an institutional routine. Reminiscence is thus subsumed within the supervisory aspect of care, and serves to reproduce its disempowering effects.

Reformulating reminiscence practice

Of course, as Bornat makes clear, this state of affairs is 'regrettable' for proponents of reminiscence, since one of the attractions of reminiscence work is its empowering potential. However, she also suggests that it is 'perhaps inevitable'. We would argue that this inevitability is not merely a function of institutional inertia, or the lack of commitment of carers in 'some institutions', but that it is in the very nature of care provision. The variable representation of reminiscence as empowering or disempowering is an embodiment of the 'dilemma of care' as both service and supervision.

This dilemma, then, constitutes a fundamental problem for the democratizing aims of reminiscence work. However, such an analysis should not be taken as pessimistic. First, it allows us to locate the source of the problem in the nature of the care relationship, rather than in the nature of particular institutions or care workers. Second, the problem itself can act as a spur to the reformulation of reminiscence practice. This is evident in extract 6, also taken from Bornat's paper:

Extract 6
Amongst the best and most committed carers, interests lie in de-routinising reminiscence activities . . . Some have become part-time researchers into memorabilia and local history . . . In some homes and hospitals, knowledge of individual past lives has led to outings and visits, closer staff and relatives involvement and shared experiences from personal histories.

(Bornat 1989:21)

Here, in the face of the 'routinisation' of reminiscence, we see a formulation of the way forward for reminiscence work as de-routinised', as involving activities which extend beyond the bounds of institutional roles, institutional buildings and institutional relationships. Thus, the 'dilemma of care', just as it can be seen as an obstacle to the empowering potential of reminiscence work, can also be seen as fuelling its change and development, as people attempt to work around the problems it poses.

Reminiscence and therapy: dilemmas of expertise

A further set of contrary representations of reminiscence appears in a debate concerning the status of reminiscence work as 'therapy', which has recently become prominent in the reminiscence literature. This debate revolves around two representations of reminiscence: reminiscence as a 'therapy' and reminiscence as an 'ordinary activity'. These are contrary in that construing reminiscence as a therapy implies that it has 'special' therapeutic benefits, over and above those derived from ordinary activities, while construing reminiscence as an 'ordinary activity' does not have such implications.

Additionally, describing reminiscence as 'therapy' implies that it must be conducted by 'expert therapists', fully trained to maximize its therapeutic benefits. Describing it as 'ordinary activity', on the other hand, implies that no such special expertise is required to do reminiscence work.

Reminiscence practice is caught between these two positions by being variably dependent, for its continuation and legitimation, on representing itself as *both* an ordinary activity and an activity which has special 'therapeutic' effects. Both of these contrary representations can be found in writing and talk of those involved in reminiscence work. Extract 7, taken from the introduction to the Help the Aged training manual (Gibson 1989a) illustrates this dilemma:

Extract 7
The notion of being able to take an ordinary everyday process of which we are all aware, and most of us engage in, and deliberately use it to enrich the lives of older people, seized the imagination of people whose day to day work in residential homes, day centres and hospitals, often lacked sparkle, excitement and rewarding relationships. The spontaneous, enthusiastic response of older people who were invited to join reminiscence groups proved irresistibly infectious. The idea of therapeutic reminiscence, or more grandly reminiscence therapy, legitimated what many older people and their carers were already doing and finding rewarding.

(Gibson 1989a:7)

Here, the ordinary status of reminiscence as an 'everyday process' is of central importance to reminiscence as practice. The notion of deliberately using this 'ordinary everyday process' was what 'seized the imagination' of care workers, and received 'enthusiastic response' from older people. The final sentence of this extract, however, hints at the problem referred to above. The title of 'therapy' as it is presented here is more than a mere afterthought in the context of an activity which people were 'already doing and finding re-warding'. First, it 'legitimated' the activity, and legitimation is more than a mere adjunct to practice; indeed, it may be essential for its continuation. Second, the 'therapy' label confers not only legitimacy, but also *grandness* – therapy is by definition a grand, special, *extra-ordinary* activity. The very act of legitimation through designation as therapy thus threatens to undermine the essential attraction of reminiscence as an *ordinary* activity.

What is the attraction of 'ordinariness'? This can be seen in extract 8, taken from an interview with a regional administrator, one of whose tasks is to supervise the provision of reminiscence resources for elderly people (*transcription key:* / = short pause):

Extract 8
Certainly I find when I do talks to care assistants/they get frightened when you say go and do reminiscence therapy/but if you say to them well look there are a load of resources here which can encourage people to get talking about their past and these are some techniques you can use in setting a group up/these are some things you need to look out for while you're running the group but you can actually do it/if you put it into the er/mystique of therapy then you're destroying it people's potential confidence

Here, the problem is clearly stated: to say reminiscence work is 'therapy' is to confer on it a 'mystique' of expert knowledge and extra-ordinary skill, which intimidates and destroys the confidence of potential practitioners, who tend to occupy the lower levels of the institutional hierarchy. Thus, it is important for the continuation and dissemination of reminiscence practice that it remains free of this mystique, as an *ordinary* process whose ordinariness affords a commonsense 'licence to practice'.

However, this move to distance reminiscence from the 'mystique of therapy', and to assert its ordinariness, also threatens to undermine its legitimacy as practice. If reminiscence work involves merely an 'ordinary everyday process', on what grounds can it justify its existence as an arena of practice? Just such a critique has been levelled at reminiscence work by clinical psychologists who, as 'therapeutic experts', may well feel bound to resist the designation of an 'ordinary everyday process' as therapy (e.g. Thornton and Brotchie 1987), since this may undermine their own claim to therapeutic expertise. Extract 9, taken from an interview with a practising clinical psychologist, is an example of such a position:

Extract 9
Got to see things for what they really are/if reminiscence therapy is a device for entertaining people you might as well be explicit about it/destroy the mysticism mystique surrounding it/the exclusivity sur-rounding it/or the arrogance surrounding it/there may be other ways of entertaining people than er constantly looking at er pictures of er some city as it was fifty years ago or what happened in the war maybe other ways

Like the previous example, this extract expresses a reluctance to designate reminiscence as therapy, and also refers to the need to avoid the 'mystique' associated with the term. However, the work being done is quite different. Whereas extract 8 is presenting a strategy for the *continuation* of practice, this extract is implicitly arguing for its *discontinuation*. Reminiscence is first trivialized as 'a device for entertaining people', and then demoted even as entertainment – 'there may be *other* ways of entertaining people' – the implication being that there may be *better* ways, which might usefully displace reminiscence. Such a construction does more than simply construe remi-niscence as ordinary, non-expert activity. It marginalizes reminiscence, by threatening its legitimacy as a practice of any special significance.

The reluctance on the part of both proponents and critics of reminiscence work to designate reminiscence as 'therapy' also stems from its implications for the practitioner–client relationship. Construing reminiscence as an 'ordinary everyday process', as well as making it accessible to non-expert practitioners, also makes it accessible to their elderly clients. It has the effect of 'democratiz-ing' the practitioner–client relationship, in that both have equal knowledge of the 'ordinary everyday process' in which they are involved. This is clearly part of the attraction of reminiscence work, as we argued in the previous section. The practitioner–client relationship of 'therapy' as expert practice, however, is inherently *unequal*, with the expert by definition having access to knowledge which the client is not party to. Thus, the 'democratic ordinariness' of reminiscence threatens to undermine the standing of the expert therapist, while the 'inegalitarian mystique' of therapy threatens to undermine the potentially democratizing attractions of reminiscence work.

The need to ensure the continuation and legitimation of practice, then, sets up a dilemma for the proponents and exponents of reminiscence work. On the one hand, they wish to claim that it has certain 'therapeutic' features which raise it above the status of entertainment; on the other, they may want it to remain ordinary and accessible for practitioners and participants alike. The variable representation of reminiscence as 'therapy' or 'ordinary activity' in discourse about reminiscence can be seen as an embodiment of practical attempts to deal with this dilemma.

Concluding comments: the need for evidence

Our discussion of the debate about the status of reminiscence as therapy brings us back to the problem with which we opened this chapter: the discrepancy between anecdote and evidence. The critique of reminiscence work referred to above hinges in part on the lack of 'hard' evidence to back up anecdotal claims for its 'therapeutic' benefits, and reports of self-evident enjoyment on the parts of participants. However, as we have indicated, the variable designation of reminiscence as 'therapy' or 'ordinary activity' is not simply a matter of research evidence, but rather reflects people's attempts to work around dilemmas which arise from the linking of reminiscence work with therapeutic expertise. From this point of view, one can see the lack of 'reliable' evidence concerning the benefits of reminiscence being used to counter moves which threaten to erode the standing of professional experts, such as clinical psychologists. This situation is compounded by the fact that the claim for the precedence of 'hard evidence' over 'anecdotal reports' is itself a function of expert practice, in that hard evidence is produced by means of expert 'scientific' practice, while anecdotal reports are frequently the subjective accounts of non-experts.

It is common to find in the reminiscence literature and in practitioners' talk, a position which defers resolution of the 'evidence problem' to the findings of future research, while at the same time asserting the 'obvious' appeal and value of reminiscence (Bornat 1989; Gibson 1989a; Norris 1989). The following quote, taken from the Help the Aged training manual, is an example of such a position:

> ... [W]e have in reminiscence work an approach which has wide immediate spontaneous appeal. This must not be lost, minimised or dismissed while we await the outcome of rigorous research studies. We know from experience that reminiscence 'works' for many older people. Herein lies its appeal and its scarcely yet explored possibilities.
>
> (Gibson 1989a:53)

We would suggest that this reliance on the outcome of 'rigorous research studies' is misplaced if it looks to current research approaches, which depend on unitary 'operational definitions' of reminiscence, and which formulate its benefits in individual psychological terms. That representations of reminiscence in the talk and writing of those in the field revolve around social-relational concerns is a consequence of reminiscence groups being arenas of social activity.

Just as current research approaches fail to address the way 'reminiscence' is defined and redefined in relation to social concerns, so they fail to address the social interactional processes which constitute reminiscence groups. In general, current research leaves these processes unanalysed. At worst, the group process is ignored completely, with psychological measures being taken from people before and after participation; at best, measures of the 'social behaviour' are taken during participation (Middleton and Buchanan 1993). But reminiscence groups are made up primarily of *talk*, and in order to understand what is going on in such groups, and in what way it is that they 'work', whatever rigorous research that is done needs to address itself to that talk. A discourse analytic perspective offers a means of studying empirically the social activity which constitutes reminiscence groups. It allows us to study talk in such groups as constructive and pragmatic action, through which a variety of purposes might be accomplished: giving people's accounts of past experience significance as part of an evolving group agenda; relocating individual problems of ageing or institutional life as part of 'common experience'; or relocating individual participants as 'members' (Middleton and Buchanan 1991; Middleton *et al.* 1991; Buchanan and Middleton 1993). Such work brings to the analysis of reminiscence work a concern for the organization of talk that has received attention within other studies of older persons' talk (see, for example, Boden and Bielby 1983, 1986; Coupland *et al.* 1991).

In the above discussions, we have tried to show that reminiscence work is a profoundly *social* phenomenon; what 'reminiscence' is taken to be, and what its benefits for older people are taken to be, are formulated and reformulated according to social-relational concerns – the social position of older people, the care relationship, and relations of expertise and equality. Reminiscence work is fundamentally concerned with the rights of older people to have a *voice* in their relations with others, and the issues we have discussed are essentially concerned with struggles to give or withhold that right to a voice. Research approaches which reduce reminiscence to an individual psychological process, with individual psychological benefits, marginalize the sociality of the reminiscence enterprise. This has the consequence of denying voice both to older people who participate in groups and to the practitioners who seek to identify and characterize just what it is about reminiscence that 'works' for them.

We have aimed to show that a discourse analytic perspective offers the possibility of studying reminiscence as a socially located, rather than merely psychological, phenomenon. In analysing the formulation and reformulation of the nature of 'reminiscence' in discourse, we can study the cultural arguments that give form to the emergence and development of reminiscence work. Discourse analysis *socializes* the agenda of reminiscence research, and offers the possibility of elucidating what practitioners mean when they say that reminiscence 'works'.

Acknowledgements

We are particularly grateful for the comments of Joanna Bornat and Faith Gibson in developing the argument of this chapter. The continuing critical discussions with members of the Discourse and Rhetoric Group at Loughborough University (including Malcolm Ashmore, Mick Billig, Derek Edwards and Jonathan Potter) have been most helpful.

6

Beyond anti-ageism: Reminiscence groups and the development of anti-discriminatory social work education and practice

_____ JOHN HARRIS AND TOM HOPKINS _____

Introduction

The need to develop anti-discriminatory practice has been given a high priority in both the curriculum design and the operational evaluation of social work education and training (Jordan 1990). Changes in social work education and training in the early 1990s have brought prejudice, disadvantage, discrimination and oppression to prominence as legitimate targets for social work intervention. As a consequence, the regulations and requirements for the national Diploma in Social Work professional qualification stipulate that social workers must be able to:

- develop an awareness of the inter-relationship of the processes of structural oppression, race, class and gender;
- understand and counteract the impact of stigma and discrimination on grounds of poverty, age, disability and sectarianism;
- recognise the need for and seek to promote policies and practices which are non-discriminatory and anti-oppressive.

(CCETSW 1991:16)

As far as ageism is concerned, a set of guidance notes on how the Diploma in Social Work curriculum might address work with older people emphasizes the importance of all students, regardless of their eventual job destination, understanding 'age discrimination particularly with regard to social policy and social work practice' (CCETSW 1992:11).

A possible consequence of these imperatives is likely to be the reconsideration of existing methods and models of practice which seem to offer ways of addressing the social division of 'age'. Given the well-established existence of group-based reminiscence, especially in the residential and day-care fields, it seems likely that social work educators, students and practice teachers may turn with renewed enthusiasm to this particular form of work with older people. The curriculum guidance notes to which we have referred envisage this possibility in suggesting that students could have their understanding of older people's rights and aspirations assessed by requiring them to describe what they have learned from participation in a reminiscence group (CCETSW 1992:12–13).

Existing support for student involvement in a 'tradition' of organized group-based reminiscence has been subjected to little critical attention. It is therefore likely to have considerable appeal as a base on which to build more rigorous attention to 'age' and 'ageism' in anti-discriminatory social work education. Accounts of reminiscence work suggest that it has this potential to counter aspects of ageism. For example, Coleman uses Dobrof's account to chart the shift in practice which the legitimation of reminiscence brought about. In the 1960s, the tendency to reminisce:

> . . . was seen as an understandable, although not entirely healthy, preoccupation with happier times, understandable because these old and infirm people walked daily in the shadow of death. At worst, 'living in the past' was viewed as pathology-regression to the dependency of the child, denial of the passage of time and the reality of the present or evidence of organic impairment of the intellect. It was even said that 'remembrance of things past' could cause or deepen depression among our residents. In a profound sense, Butler's writings [on life review] liberated both the old and the nurses, doctors and social workers; the old were free to remember, to regret, to look reflectively at the past and try to understand it. And we were free to listen, and to treat rememberers and remembrance with the respect they deserved.
>
> (Dobrof, quoted in Coleman 1986:9–10)

Given the evident appeal of a method of work addressing the social division of 'age' in the way Dobrof describes, we have witnessed a situation in which 'the pendulum has swung completely round and reminiscence forms one of the most popular approaches to therapeutic and diversionary work with older people, particularly in residential settings' (Coleman 1991:126). The prospect of even more widespread use of organized reminiscence groups in the future, with a more explicitly anti-discriminatory focus, suggests that this is perhaps an appropriate point at which to assess the potential contribution of such groups.

In this chapter, we set out to question the extent to which much of the group-based reminiscence in residential and day-care settings may be seen as providing an adequate conceptual and practice foundation for anti-discriminatory social work practice with older people. We will argue that notwithstanding the obvious and widespread appeal of reminiscence groups, there are inherent dangers in regarding much group-based reminiscence, as presently conceived and practised in the examples we have encountered, is self-evidently anti-ageist and anti-discriminatory. We will argue that to play its part in the promotion of anti-discriminatory practice, reminiscence groupwork needs to be subjected to review and evaluation in the light of changing social realities for older people and the impact of other social divisions on their lives.

The reminiscence tradition in social work

Social work texts endorse reminiscence in one-to-one work with older people, echoing the benefits outlined in Butler's much-quoted article in which he advocated the value of undertaking life-review (Butler 1963). For example, the social work literature considers the usefulness of reminiscence: in putting an older person's life in perspective (Mortimer 1982:59; Scrutton 1989:105; Froggatt 1990:66); in locating the origins of current problems and helping to resolve them (Rowlings 1981:63; Mortimer 1982:59; Scrutton 1989:104); and in rediscovering and reinforcing a sense of personal identity (Rowlings 1981:61; Scrutton 1989:103).

However, the benefits of reminiscence have been more popularly promoted in forms of practice which go beyond the one-to-one work originally proposed by Butler and espoused in social work texts. The form of practice with which we are particularly concerned is organized group-based reminiscence in residential and day-care settings as it has been group-based reminiscence, rather than work with individuals, which has been the dominant form of practice in these settings. Like all forms of groupwork, group-based reminiscence varies according to the setting, clientele, worker's style and the available resources. However, we believe, based on our experience of contact with this form of work, that there are common features in evidence in a wide range of groups which have as their starting points slide or card sets, videos and artefacts as stimuli to older people's reminiscence.

Such groups are usually offered on a voluntary basis to service users and will occupy some 1–1½ hours weekly. Wherever possible, workers will try and ensure that groups take place in comfortable surroundings familiar to residents/members. Groups will vary in size from perhaps three or four to a dozen older people. It is common practice to offer such groups to those who seem most able to benefit. Usually, potential members are 'screened' by staff for their capacity to participate in collective activities. The extent of cognitive, visual and hearing impairments may be of significance here.

Most groups will be led by one worker, often a student or junior staff member, who will make use of materials and objects supplied in pre-packaged 'reminiscence kits' (see Table 6.1). Such staff may have received some training for their role; most often they will not, their expertise coming from a combination of observing other workers, reading and practice supervision.

While the above can only be a partial picture of what constitutes a burgeoning area of reminiscence groupwork with older people, it very much reflects that which we have encountered in our work as social work educators, and specifically in our roles as tutors engaged in the planning and monitoring of placements for social work students. Both in the setting up and observation of our students' work over nearly a decade, we have been afforded the opportunity to discuss with them and their practice teachers issues relating to reminiscence groupwork.

Through our individual and joint experiences and activities in the field, we have come to a strong appreciation of the motives and ethos that underpin

Table 6.1   Examples of reminiscence kits

Flashback Postcards (postcard set): Winslow Press
Lifetimes (photograph set): Winslow Press
Recall (tape/slide set): Help the Aged
Newsreel Trivia (video/quiz): Winslow Press
Video Reminiscence (40 videos, each based on a specific year): Winslow Press
Sounds Nostalgic (cassette-tape set): Winslow Press
Happy as a Sandboy (set of railway posters): Winslow Press
Union Jack (items from British Forces newspapers): Winslow Press
Maps for Reminiscence (British Isles, World Maps): Winslow Press
Reminiscing 1950s–1980s (board game): Winslow Press

much group-based reminiscence. We understand the obvious attractions – for service users and workers alike – of a method that appears to offer an easily managed therapeutic intervention. However, it is through these same experiences that we have been persuaded of the need to look critically at group-based reminiscence, and in particular at some of the key claims made for it, both as a therapeutic or diversionary method and for its contribution to anti-discriminatory practice. It is precisely because we believe that reminiscence has much to offer to the older people *and* that it requires review and reconceptualization that we wish to share the ideas and observations that follow.

Reconsidering group-based reminiscence

Bromley explains the advantages of reminiscence in group care settings in terms of working with the loss of a 'a sense of personal identity because of relocation or institutionalisation' (Bromley 1988:278). Reminiscence groups are said to offer three-fold benefits: to the older person as an individual; to older people collectively; and to the staff who work with older people.

The benefits to older people have been identified as recreational, pyschological and therapeutic (Norris 1986). Reminiscence has been regarded as stressing the assets of an older person, emphasizing individuality and identity and, by so doing, promoting a sense of self-worth (Norris 1986; Scrutton 1989). Older people are also considered to gain benefits from reminiscence through its impact on communication patterns; shared memories leading to more interaction, of a more intimate nature (Bornat 1985). The value of encouraging reminiscence by older people as far as staff are concerned is located in the insights provided into older people's formative years, insights which can be used in understanding current problems and uncertainties (Carter 1981–82; Martin 1989; Scrutton 1989; Eleftheriades 1991).

These benefits of group-based reminiscence presumably account for the existing strong support for such groups we have encountered in our work as social work tutors, when negotiating the content of students' group focused practice in residential and day-care placements. In these settings, students are almost always involved in running a reminiscence group. Many practice teachers seem to regard such groups as a relatively simple, structured approach to therapeutic work with older people which can be adapted to the student's needs and level of experience and to the needs of the service users. In particular, reminiscence offers students a ready-made therapeutic kit with which to counteract any tendency to regard social work in group care settings as simply 'warehousing' (Miller and Gwynne 1979).

Before considering how work with reminiscence groups might respond to requirements concerning the development of anti-discriminatory practice, we consider three notes of caution concerning assumptions about the nature of older people's memory and the value reminiscence has for them. First, there has tended to be an assumption that reminiscence work is, in part, a humane means of dealing with older people's inability to store and retrieve recent memories, whereas it may be that for an older person reminiscence is a means of dealing with an uneventful present. A study by Holland and Rabbitt (1991) highlights the inadvisability of divorcing an older person's memory from its function. They suggest that for older people in residential care, talking about the past becomes more important, both for entertainment and to maintain a sense of identity in the communal environment. Using individual testing in a comparison of active older people living in the community and residents of homes for older people, Holland and Rabbitt discovered that the residents produced more early than recent memories, whereas the active older people living in the community remembered not only more overall but also more of what they remembered consisted of recent occurrences. Holland and Rabbitt regard it as likely that older people in residential care spend more time reminiscing about earlier events because the social context of their current life situation has an important effect on their memory, rather than their memory simply being a function of their age.

If the setting has an influence on memory in the way suggested by this study, it may be that the older people make the necessary 'situational adjustment' (Becker 1964; Baldwin *et al.* 1993) required by their participation in a reminiscence group, to a repertoire of other situational adjustments: for example, adopting a distant or jocular demeanour during the performance of intimate care; being minimally sociable in the lounge, but aggressive in defence of personal space, if necessary; being 'settled' in the home when relatives call. Further, if reminiscence is one of the few stimulating experiences on offer, its significance to older people may be distorted by the lack of available alternatives. In such a situation, reminiscence is likely to stand out from the potential barrenness of institutional everyday life.

In one of the few research-based accounts of a reminiscence group, Fielden found that a reminiscence group produced more and different patterns of communication among its members, whereas a 'here and now' control group had no effect of this kind (Fielden 1990). The 'here and now' group was, however, concerned with health promotion. It is possible that a here and now discussion group concerned with contemporary issues of direct relevance to older people's lives – for example, government plans for the National Health Service – might have produced very different results.

Secondly, all this suggests that the increasingly prevalent view that reminiscence is good for older people en masse, common in our encounters with reminiscence groups, needs to be challenged. It seems to us that, in the emergent practice orthodoxy, reluctance to reminisce may be seen as an indication of a pathological condition rather than an expression of individual choice.

Coleman's study is helpful here in identifying four sets of attitudes toward reminiscence; reminiscers who find it helpful or disturbing and non-reminiscers for whom it seems pointless or depressing (Coleman 1986:3, 153). The increasingly prevalent assumption communicated to students in practice placements by practitioners that reminiscence is a necessary part of ageing for all older people needs much closer scrutiny: 'Reminiscence can be a sign of successful ageing and high morale, and so can the absence of reminiscence' (Coleman 1991:133)

Thirdly, reminiscence groups may encourage those working with older people to be more respectful, but they may also lock older people into the stereotypical role of 'sage' (for an exploration of the dynamics of this process, see Biggs 1990:3–4). This stereotyping is pervasive and is evident even in attempts to develop more critical and radical forms of practice:

> [The older person's] information comes in an extremely rambling form, repeating itself again and again and not easily providing a picture of anything but a fragmented reality. To go beyond this, the social worker must play an active part in the interaction: he [*sic*] must intervene in the conversation to structure it beyond a monologue, to press for information in a genuine way. Thus the interaction is not between a boring monologue from an old person who is going through the motions of conversation and a social worker who is bored and wanting to leave: it becomes an active conversation from someone with some form of knowledge and a person new to the area who needs it. The old person in this interaction is useful to the social worker . . .
>
> (Corrigan and Leonard 1978:59)

Given the difficulties faced by workers with older people 'in which the cornerstone of social encounter becomes shaky, if not completely dislodged' (Biggs 1990:51), the sense of purpose gained by the worker from respectfully unleashing the contribution of the 'sage' is likely to be profound. While conferring a positive attribute on older people, and thus contributing to the countering of discrimination, regarding them as 'sages' may lock them into a role in which their memories are predominant and aspects of their current lives are not accorded sufficient attention.

Reminiscence groups and anti-discriminatory practice

Workers operating within reminiscence groups may have a general belief, articulated to a greater or lesser extent, that they are combating an ageism which is rooted in the marginalization and devaluation of 'older people' by 'society'. Such a sweeping definition of ageism is in itself problematic (Bytheway and Johnson 1990:34–35), but in the context of developing anti-discriminatory practice it reinforces a view of the need to develop forms of practice capable of combating each of the specific 'isms'. This approach to the disaggregation of social divisions, implied by much reminiscence work needs to be questioned.

For example, class as a social division is implicitly at the heart of many organized reminiscence groups which are ostensibly focused on 'age' in the sense that such groups consist predominantly of white, working-class users of services, most often in group care settings. Work in these groups tends to portray white, working-class older people as 'victims', albeit victims who have radiated heroic fortitude in the wretched social and economic circumstances of their earlier lives. The emphasis is on their sense of solidarity in hardship, in previous times and now recaptured, in the face of adversities such as mass unemployment. This is reinforced by treating the experience of the Second World War through the dominant theme of social, economic and political unity summed up in the evocative phrase 'the war effort'. Inadequate and punitive state welfare provision of bygone times is set against more recent 'social progress' and the relative absence of hardship in their present lives. (For a discussion of the perpetuation of consensus views of the past through group recollection, see Bornat 1992, 1993.)

However, in speaking to a supposedly shared experience of 'age', this cohort approach may ignore issues of 'race', gender, class and sexuality. In other words, in tackling ageism through reminiscence groupwork, 'age' has been seen as the dominant system of social relations which shapes reminiscence. Rather than adopting a broader analysis capable of examining the *interlocking* nature of social divisions, membership of one social division – 'age' – excludes, or virtually excludes, the significance of membership of others. Yet on the evidence available concerning the significance of 'race' (Norman 1985; Thomas 1990), class (Estes 1979; Townsend 1981; Walker 1981; Phillipson 1982; Thompson 1992) and gender (Evers 1981; Hemmings 1983; Peace 1986; Ford and Sinclair 1987; Arber and Ginn 1991) 'age' may not be the only, or even the primary, social division shaping older people's circumstances and experiences.

The lack of attention to a range of social divisions in reminiscence groupwork of the type we have described is thus unhelpful in developing a broadly based anti-discriminatory practice. It obscures the ways in which 'race', class, gender and sexuality are embedded in the construction of varying forms and experiences of 'old age' through denying the significance of these social divisions in earlier life. Our experience suggests that where reminiscence groups touch on social divisions other than age, for example on gender through discussion of artefacts of domestic labour, such social divisions are seen as having mediated a general experience of 'life' rather than having directly shaped individual life-experience.

In adopting a cohort approach of the type we have described much reminiscence groupwork seems to assume that memory – individual or collective – simply exists. Events are simply remembered, or they are not. Billig argues that this is far from the case:

> ... the collective processes which enable memorisation to occur will themselves be part of wider ideological patterns. That being so, investigators should seek to locate the ways in which ideological forces affect, and indeed constitute, the psychological processes of memory.
>
> However, the relations between ideology and memory will not be causally one way, with preformed ideology impinging upon individual psychology. Ideology itself will be a form of social memory, in as much as it constitutes what collectively is remembered and also what is forgotten or

what aspects of society's history continue to be commemorated and what are relegated to the unread archives.

(Billig 1989:60)

Billig's argument (and see also Crawford *et al.* 1992) is an important one in the context of reminiscence. The form and content of reminiscence groups we have encountered, and the experiences evoked by them, are most often regarded as ideologically neutral. Such approaches ignore the extent to which social structure and the experience of social divisions have shaped, and still shape, the life-course of older people, especially the constraints placed on their expectations and personality development by ideological forces and their experience of social divisions:

The problems of ageing are differentially experienced, according to class, gender and race and influenced critically by continuities in the distribution of material rewards and opportunities for power and personal development earlier in life.

(Bowl 1981:56)

However, as Leonard (1984) emphasizes, the operation of ideological forces is not unilinear, but is characterized by tensions, contradictions and resistance. For example, reminiscence groups which stress the commonality of (white working-class) people's wartime experiences, and the solidarity in evidence at that time, may unwittingly touch on other important features of the period, such as continued class antagonisms, industrial strife and conflictual gender relations.

It is in these respects that we are concerned that much contemporary reminiscence groupwork will not provide an adequate foundation for the development of anti-discriminatory practice. Students – and others – running reminiscence groups may have unwittingly focused on 'technical' issues of materials and presentation to the exclusion of any real consideration of the ideological context and content of organized reminiscence. The way in which stimulus materials are employed is usually largely determined by the worker. Thus, reminiscence groupwork runs the risk of being, or becoming, a process in which the selection, deployment and evaluation of materials is very much in the hands of service providers and very little in the control of service users. This tendency is in conflict with the alleged change in power relations which reminiscence work is said to bring about (Carter 1981–82; Scrutton 1989). This is not to argue that such pre-selection of materials by workers is necessarily against the best interests of older people, but rather to raise the possibility of alternative approaches.

For example, the life-history approach has been used by some social gerontologists in their research (Johnson 1976, 1986; Johnson *et al.* 1980; di Gregorio 1986, 1987). It is an approach which has the capacity to bring together both the impact of a range of social divisions on older people's lives, past and present, and also the variety of influences Coleman identifies as acting on the construction of an individual's life-history: personality, culture, major turning points, the search for meaning, the need to explain and defend actions (Coleman 1991:120). It appears to have made little inroad into the examples of reminiscence groupwork we have encountered.

One approach to the use of life-histories in reminiscence groups is on offer from the USA in the form of 'guided autobiography' (Birren and Deutchman 1991). This involves the formulation and sharing of accounts of who group members are and where they have come from. Birren and Deutchman (1991) suggest that their approach promotes *systematic* reminiscence concerning the shaping of self and life circumstances and contrast this with more spontaneous forms of reminiscence, such as that with which we have been concerned in this chapter.

If older people are offered more opportunity to shape the content and process of their reminiscing (see Chapters 8, 10 and 11, this volume), at least some may choose very different events and activities from those available in a pre-packaged form, extensively tested though these may have originally been. As a result of adopting a more reflexive and open approach to the selection of reminiscence content, it is also possible that older people may come to radically different conclusions both about which past experiences they regard as important and also about the sense they now make both of their history and their present lives.

Social work students may find that, offered such opportunities, older people's views of their experiences and of past events in general may not add up to a coherent and conflict-free whole, but rather remain fragmented, ambiguous and troublesome for them and their carers. These 'alternative accounts' may not surface immediately or directly during reminiscence sessions. They may be visited on those least aware of their origins in the reminiscence work taking place, for example, volunteers, care staff and relatives.

Conclusion

Organized reminiscence groups in residential and day-care settings run the danger of implicitly reinforcing aspects of ageist attitudes towards older people, by confirming a narrow view of them as conservatively preoccupied with personal memories and collective expressions of nostalgia. However, paying attention to the ideological dimensions of reminiscence work does not mean abandoning its central tenet – that older people may benefit from being assisted in remembering earlier periods, events and people in their lives. Nevertheless, as Phillipson suggests, a starting-point for developing anti-discriminatory practice lies in beginning to challenge 'those ideological forces that help to justify and maintain marginal status' (Phillipson 1989:199).

If reminiscence groupwork is, in the future, to retain its prominent position in the field of work with older people in forms which contribute to the development of anti-discriminatory practice, its purposes and concerns need to be reconsidered. Hitherto, a predominantly consensual view of the welfare state as the culmination of post-war social and economic progress, has influenced the content, process and outcome of cohort reminiscence group-work. This may soon be replaced by a very different set of political and social realities as possible contexts for reminiscence by new cohorts. Greater geographical mobility, changing social and occupational expectations among women, increasing numbers of Black and other minority group elders and successive New Right governments are but a few of the features of late twentieth-century life that will be likely to form part of the individual and collective memories of older people as they reminisce in the late twentieth and early twenty-first centuries. If reminiscence work is to contribute to the development of anti-discriminatory practice, it needs to begin from the ambiguities, tensions and contradictions of older people's earlier lives and it must allow the possibility of older people reflecting on their past and contemporary experiences and interpreting them in new and different ways.

7

A fair hearing: Life-review in a hospital setting

Introduction

The development of the tape/slide presentation *Recall* in 1981, encouraged a widespread interest in the use of reminiscence activities with older people in Britain. Once the explicit support of the national charity Help the Aged had been given to the process of encouraging older people to share their memories, care workers felt empowered to challenge the view that promoting reminiscence was inevitably harmful. In my own experience as a nurse, reminiscence seemed to offer benefits to both patients and staff. Patients enjoyed the opportunity to relive their memories of working-class life in South London through the medium of photographs, wall posters and records of music hall songs. For some people, remembering in groups seemed to act as a stimulus to the retrieval of memories and to the development of lasting bonds with their fellow patients. Others clearly felt more comfortable when recounting their experiences on an individual basis. Nursing staff found that reminiscence activities provided information about the life-experiences of patients which helped to explain their present attitudes and tastes. So the discovery that one woman who seemed to be obsessed with the standard of cleaning achieved by the domestic staff on the ward had spent her working life as a cleaner in a wide range of government buildings, including Number 10 Downing Street, helped to transform resentment into a lively interest. Similarly, discovering that a patient who was terrified of hospital staff had once been a prisoner in the Theresienstadt camp made us more sensitive to her fears and anxious to find ways to minimize them.

For patients such as these, reminiscence activities seemed to provide at best new insight into their lives which could be used to provide more sensitive nursing interventions, and at worst a harmless stimulus for conversation. As experience was gained in this new approach, it gradually became apparent that there were some for whom reminiscence did not appear to be helpful. One woman ruminated obsessively on the loss of her husband during the Nazi era in Austria, and encouraging reminiscence only seemed to compound this process. Another patient who had been brought up in Germany at the turn of the century, but who had fled to Britain to escape from the Nazi regime, was upset by a wall poster from the First World War, as it awakened memories of the anti-German hostility she had encountered during the 'Phoney' War.

The publication of the results of Coleman's longitudinal study of interviews with the residents of a sheltered housing scheme in London served to confirm a more qualified approach to reminiscence (Coleman 1986). So it became increasingly difficult to sustain the view that reminiscence was a universal experience which could be enjoyed by all. The memories of many people encompass guilt, regret or a sense of failure. Some harbour anger because of the way they have been treated in the past, while others have unresolved grief.

Coleman's work emphasizing the complexity of individual views of the past gave pause for reflection in the prevailing climate of optimism, but certainly mirrored my own experience of listening to reminiscence. It seemed to me that the situation was analogous to that of the discovery of a new drug. It was clear that something important had been discovered, but it was not immediately apparent what form it would take, or what practical use it could be put to.

In health care, much biographical material was already obtained for the purposes of establishing the past medical and nursing histories and the social situation in which the older person lived. The challenge for nurses working in institutional settings seemed to be to develop conceptual tools which would enable them to make direct use of biographical material. The 'Gloucester Project' initiated by the Open University and the Policy Studies Institute showed how this might be attempted when assessing the care needs of older people living in the community (Johnson *et al.* 1988). However, as Haight (1991) has argued, much more systematic knowledge of the types and processes of reminiscence is required before application of the information gained will be possible. It is clear that group reminiscence must be separated from individual life-review and structured approaches distinguished from unstructured ones. The situation is further complicated by the fact that, as Cornwell and Gearing (1989:42) have argued, 'everybody has several life stories or versions of the same story'.

Coleman (1986:4) has presented persuasive arguments in favour of developing case study material for the development of knowledge of reminiscence, and this is the approach which I have chosen for this chapter. The use of case studies in the medical sciences literature has proved to be a powerful tool for the elucidation of the features of disease processes. By its very nature, reminiscence represents a person's individual account of his or her own life, so a method of transmission which preserves as much as possible of the authentic voice has much to commend it.

As Coleman points out, a case study approach may involve bias, as the reader has no means of checking the summary against the original evidence. With the rapid development of compact disc technology, it may soon be possible to publish recordings of reminiscence material, but until that time it is necessary to transcribe them. Transcription from tape-recording also presents problems, as complete accuracy with regard to the sounds on the tape renders the transcription unreadable:

> I . . . I mean we . . . er . . . [clears throat] . . . er . . . used to play . . . you know, like children do, 'cos this would have been about, well I'm not, yes must have been 1926 or around then . . .

In the case studies which follow, an attempt has been made to render the tape-recordings as faithfully as possible given the limitations of this approach.

Watt and Wong (1991) have recently attempted to develop a taxonomy of reminiscence as a first step in the development of therapeutic uses for such memories. Their taxonomy classifies six types of reminiscence: integrative, instrumental, transmissive, narrative, escapist and obsessive. They further identify eleven major themes of reminiscence: childhood memories, dating and marriage, domestic life, children and grandchildren, significant others (including relatives and friends), education and career (including personal accomplishments), societal events, health, relocation, death and existential beliefs (including religious or philosophical beliefs regarding life and death). Each person in their study was interviewed by a researcher, and the audio-tape was then analysed by two people who scored it on the basis of the number of words devoted to each type and each theme. Watt and Wong recognize the potential pitfalls of such a mechanistic approach to content analysis by advocating a focus on segments of reminiscence, which may extend to several paragraphs in length, rather than on isolated sentences.

Watt and Wong's paper encouraged me to see if any of the types which they have identified could be applied to three interviews which I conducted several years ago in a hospital ward for elderly people in South London. At the time I believed that reminiscence was a straightforward activity that involved asking a series of questions of an older person in order to establish what the past had *really* been like in that part of London. On such terms, these interviews seemed to be failures as they contained very little information on local history. I felt that I had lost control of the interview process and been given material which was clearly important to the interviewees but which made little sense to me. It was not until a more sophisticated understanding of the reminiscence process began to be developed by Watt and Wong, among others, that it seemed to be worthwhile to return to them.

Case study 1

Mrs A had been a patient on the hospital ward for some time before I was able to record an interview with her. She had watched the development of reminiscence activities on the ward with interest, but the effects of heart disease prevented her from taking an active part. In one of the remissions shortly before her death, Mrs A agreed to talk to me about her life:

> I was born in Queen Charlotte's Hospital, 1910, and I only had one parent. I was illegitimate, and my mum was the one that had to take care of me. My mother was needing a very serious operation, and they used to have people come in – like ladies – to choose who they would take to look after, while the mother was undergoing an operation. According to what I

can remember, she had a lovely face, this very old lady, but she was a *real* lady. It appears that she had me out in the pram one day, and a gentleman was passing by. He came back and looked in the pram again and said to her, 'This isn't your baby.'

So she said, 'No, I know I am too old, it's from the Unmarried Mothers.'

He said, 'Do you know, she's the complete image of my baby that I lost, together with my poor wife in childbirth. Do you think that the mother would let me adopt her?'

So she said, 'Well, that's not for me to say.'

Anyway, when she went back she spoke to my mum and she said 'On no account' – so that all dropped through.

Eventually of course I came out with my mum, and there was an aunt – one of my mum's sisters – Aunt Polly. She was very much in debt to my mother, the way she had done away with some of my mum's money and goods that had been given into her care. So when it came to questioning about me, and my mum getting a job – my mum got a job in the Woolwich Arsenal on the TNT – this aunt said she would take care of me *providing* my mother bought all my clothes when they were needed, and she would give me food. So that's how I was signed and settled.

Time went on and went on, and I remember I had a very bad cough, and they tell me that I had whooping cough for nearly a year. I was in a really bad state.

Well my aunt lived over at Holloway, in Braes Street, and although it was only a small house, she used to let the top flat to a man and his wife. My mum said she had been in hospital again, and when she came out, she said, 'I'll go down and see Pam.'

So she started down to my aunt's turning, and they wasn't very big streets and they all knew one another, and my mum said she saw this little girl come out of this stable – no shoes on her feet or anything – and she said, 'I was puzzling and puzzling – whose child can it be?'

Anyway, lo and behold, it turned out to be me.

My mum took me into my aunt's, because they always had their doors loose then, you know, and as my mum went in, someone called out, 'Is that you Polly?'

She said, 'It's me – Jane.'

'Oh, Jane', she said, 'I am so glad I can speak to you' (this is what my mum told me she said).

'Oh, please take that child away from here, *please* – she can't go to a worse place than this. It's your sister, but by gum, she don't look after her as she ought. She said her little life is a misery, and that's why if I can get a bit of bread and butter into her, I do.'

Course, my mum was astounded. 'Not my sister Polly!', she said.

'That's true!' With that, my mother thought she couldn't leave me there another night, so she told my aunt Polly she had got somewhere else to take me – but she hadn't.

Well, my mother was living with a woman friend in Hayles Buildings, Elliot's Row, St George's Road, and it appears that they earned their living in an immoral way. So they were told to get out, and the question was with my mum, where would she put me?

Well, she was asking the neighbours if they knew of anyone, and someone suddenly came up with this lady, Mrs Jeffs. 'Oh', they said, 'Mrs Jeffs will look after her for you.'

Mrs Jeffs had two daughters, and I was put there to live, you see.

Well, time went on and I don't mind telling you that life was a misery. You can tell what it was like. The neighbours said that they thought that if they went to the Cruelty to Children Society, the Society would let *them* know, and so they were frightened. They wanted to put Mrs Jeffs away, but of course they were frightened for themselves. So anyway something happened, and they took my mum aside, but she said, 'No, I can't believe that.'

They said, 'It's true – we've heard her scream.'

(They used to have a very thin cane they used to cane me with.) Anyway it came to be that they called the family – 'the Cinderella family' – I was Cinderella, the two daughters were the ugly sisters, and the other one was [inaudible].

Things went on and on, and the people opposite – their children – used to go to a Sunday School, in a turning out of London Road in Southwark. Their mother said one day, 'Why don't you let Pam go with the children to Sunday School?'

'Oh , I don't know, I don't know.'

So it went on for a few weeks, and in the end she let me go . . . I thoroughly enjoyed it . . . It so got to me that I said I must accept the Lord as my Saviour.

Discussion

The first part of this interview has been transcribed in full because it seems to illustrate several points made in the literature on reminiscence. The most striking feature about it is that it is not a conversation about the past, and Mrs A did not require any questions in order to provide suitable prompts. The written text simply cannot convey the intensity of the experiences of making the recording. We were alone in the ward office, and Mrs A was very aware of the fact that her death was approaching and that this would probably be her last opportunity to talk about her life. As Butler (1963:67) wrote, 'the life review, Janus-like, involves facing death as well as looking back'. In a recent paper, Burnside and Haight (1992: 857) distinguish between reminiscence and life-review, and my interview with Mrs A has many of the features which they identify in the latter: it was conducted on a one-to-one basis; it contained an evaluative component; and it was used in preparation for death.

In the taxonomy proposed by Watt and Wong (1991), Mrs A's account would seem to meet their criteria for 'transmissive reminiscence', in which 'the reminiscer passes on to a younger generation some enduring values and wisdoms which s/he has acquired, growing up in a different era . . . Several of our subjects are very religious and they are eager to share with others what God has done for them in their lives' (pp. 46 and 48).

Cornwell and Gearing's (1989) contention that everyone has several versions of their life-story also seems to be relevant here. The *form* in which the account is given should also be taken into account when trying to understand what is being communicated. In the case of Mrs A, it seems that two 'literary' forms have influenced her account: one sacred and the other secular. the first is the evangelical testament, through which the believer makes public witness to the role that religion has played in her life. This form has a long history, reaching back at least to seventeenth-century puritanism (Thomas 1978:109). The second 'literary' form is the striking use of the fairy-tale motif. Explicit reference is made to Cinderella, and some of the language – 'lo and behold', 'whose child can it be?' – seems to show that influence, while the episode of the old lady with the lovely face and the gentleman who was passing by must surely be a symbolic encounter. The changeling is a common feature of fairy tales and implies that Mrs A may have been rescued into a better life. This is not to say that Mrs A's account of childhood abuse is untrue, but rather that she has chosen to convey it using forms with which she thought I would be familiar, and which may possibly help to distance her from the distressing events she was describing. This device also provided a basis for generalizing her private pain and humiliation.

Case study 2

Mrs B occupied the hospital bed next to Mrs A, and like her neighbour was facing the prospect of imminent death. She was confined to a wheelchair, following bilateral above-knee amputations. After attending a showing of the reminiscence package *Recall* and expressing pleasure at the memories which it evoked, she readily agreed to my request for a taped interview. Although the interview was conducted in a private setting, as the one with Mrs A had been, the atmosphere was completely different. Mrs B required frequent questions from me in order to prompt her replies, and there was no sense of the intensity of the confessional. Indeed, I was left with the sense of having witnessed a struggle between the two opposing facets of her character, in which the need to share her memories overcame her strong natural reserve.

Mrs B had been born in 1894 in the South London district in which she spent her whole life. I was aware of the fact that hospitals had played an important part in her autobiographical account. Her grandfather had been an inmate of a local workhouse, and she had vivid memories of the Poor Law era:

Well, there was a room where they could sit and read. Of course they had just bare boards and that, wasn't like it is today, see. But he was quite contented about it – of course he was a good age, you see, was past working.

Mrs B herself started work in 1935, in the laundry of the hospital in which she was now a patient:

There was an epidemic of 'flu, and people were dropping down with it – the hospital staff and all – and a friend of mine said to me, 'We are short of staff' she said, 'They've all been dropping down with the 'flu.'

'Well, I've had it', I says, 'And I'm going back to work next week.'

'Would you like to come and do a few days at the hospital?' she said, 'I'm sure they'd be glad of you.'

So of course with that, the next morning I went with her, and told them I would do three days . . . then course they put me on the permanent staff.

However, it soon became apparent that the Second World War was the central event in the life of Mrs B, and it was not long before she raised the topic:

I was there four years when the War broke out. We all had our orders, what to do when the warning went: of course we left work and took cover. Course there was no work getting done, so they had a meeting and they suggested we carried on working. They would have a man look out and when he blew his whistle we would take cover. So of course we all agreed we'd do that – soon as he blew his whistle we used to get down under the bench, up against the wall, and then come out when the whistle went to say it was 'all clear'. One day we got the bombing – in the day-time – they come with fire bombs and picked their targets, and in the night-time we had a terrible raid. St Giles' [Hospital] got bombed, and a coachload of soldiers – Czechoslovakians – got hit and they were all killed. They were taken into the mortuary.

The next morning the gentleman said to us, 'You needn't go, you won't be wanted, the hospital's been bombed.' But we went, and course we had to help – do anything, help to get them ready for evacuation. After we'd cleared up.

The normal hospital routines and job demarcations were erased in the aftermath of a bad air-raid, and although the laundry had been destroyed, Mrs B was kept busy in helping the casualties:

That day we got bombed at Peckham, they were fetching them in on barrows – the casualties – because they caught the Sun-Pat [factory], and course that was syrup. Some of them was dripping in syrup . . . I was hotting the kettles of water – of course we hadn't got any gas, no heating, and filling up the buckets and pails for them to wash. They were laid on stretchers until they were evacuated.

J.A.: Must have been a very distressing time?

Yes, but really you was too full of the work to get done. You didn't take a lot of notice.

Although Mrs B did not have an opportunity to acknowledge her emotions at the time, it is clear that this provided some of the motivation behind her present interest in reminiscence. She remembered some of the members of the hospital staff who had been killed, and felt that she could so easily have been among them.

Among the other memories which Mrs B wished to record was the struggle to ensure that her fellow union members received the correct wages:

The general hospitals got the extra wages, so of course everyone wanted to know when we were going to get them. So they had a union meeting, and I was picked as delegate for there.

J.A.: Which union is this?

Mine was Municipal. And I went, and course no-one stood up and said what they were there for, so in the end I did. I put me hand up, so the chairman put his hammer down, and I said 'Mr Chairman, I would just like to ask you – the general hospitals have got the increase, when are we going to get it?

He said, 'You'll get it. It will take three to four weeks, but you will get it, and with back pay.'

So I said, 'Oh thank you, Mr Chairman, that's what I want to know.'

That was it – within three weeks we got it with back pay, but of course they stopped the income tax. But I found them very fair because on one occasion after that, the supervisor went on her holidays for three weeks, and the under-supervisor, she was took sick, so of course it come to me. So 'the office' come down and told them I was in charge . . . and I got a very good recommendation. One day to my surprise, another gentleman came down to see me, and he told me he'd had a very satisfactory report, so he said, 'You're going to get the money as supervisor, plus what you've drawn', so I had a good bit to come. It come in very nicely, but it was nice to know I satisfied.

Mrs B clearly felt gratified that her supervisory abilities in the hospital laundry had been appreciated, but there was another aspect of her work which she felt more ambivalent about. This was her readiness to go out of her way to help other members of the hospital staff:

We were all out for one another – helping one another. You know sometimes, when the nurses got a break, we'd tell them. So they'd come down with their tennis clothes, [and we would] give 'em a press up for them. And some [laundry staff] would say, 'Oh, I can't do [that]. . . .' I'd say, 'For goodness sake, give them a break!' and I used to help. Then when the War was over they had a Peace Gathering, and the nurses brought down their dresses – some I washed, some I pressed, but I never went in the evening: they asked for me!

J.A.: Where was this Gathering?

At the Dulwich Hospital. Course I never went back in the evening. They asked for me – they wanted to know who had done the dresses. Course they were quite pleased about it – said how nice all the nurses looked! [But] I felt tired, time I was done of a night.

Discussion

This short passage reflects a common theme in many of my conversations with Mrs B. It was not so much that she expected gratitude or special treatment in return for the favours she had done for members of my profession during the War. It was rather that she still saw herself as a member of the hospital staff, rather than as a patient. As such, she was happy to see the slides in the *Recall* pack, but she could never be persuaded to take part in group-based reminiscence activities with other patients. Yet she was always keen to share her memories on an individual basis with members of the nursing staff.

In terms of the taxonomy created by Watt and Wong, Mrs B's account clearly had a strong thread of narrative reminiscence running through it. However, her attempt to emphasize continuities between her job in the hospital laundry and her present situation as a hospital patient would seem to fall into the category of instrumental reminiscence. She used her past experiences in the hospital service in order to help cope with the unwelcome situation in which she found herself. By identifying with the ward staff rather than with the other patients, she attempted to retain her sense of identity in the face of the losses which admission to hospital brings with it.

Case study 3

Mrs C was a ninety-year-old woman who had been admitted to the ward following an acute episode of ill-health, but her ability to cope on her own at home was in doubt after her recovery, so she remained on the ward while assessments were carried out. It soon became clear that she would not be able to return home, so arrangements were made to seek a nursing home place for her. During this long period of waiting, attempts were made to provide some activities to help pass the time and she was invited to join the reminiscence group for a showing of the *Recall* slides. As Mrs C always seemed to enjoy talking about the past, we were surprised at her angry reaction to the experience. She returned to the ward vowing never to attend the group again, and denouncing the *Recall* pack to anyone who would listen. Her anger seemed to derive from a feeling that the slides represented a hopelessly distorted view of the past, and she was particularly concerned that the student nurses who had been present should not be misled into thinking that *Recall* was fair and accurate. In view of this hostile reaction to a reminiscence experience, I was surprised when she offered to take part in the series of taped interviews which she knew that I was conducting. As she said:

> You can use some of this nonsense, but if it is anything you think that I know, I never mind telling you – if I remember it. Can't remember years – funny that! You can't remember, you don't *want* to remember, I think that's it. You push it aside, don't you? Good job that I've got nothing bad that I don't want to remember! I haven't been good, but I haven't been bad.

The transcription of my interview with Mrs C has presented particular problems because her conversation consisted of short, isolated phrases which rarely came together to form a complete sentence. A compromise has had to be arrived at between verbal accuracy and readability. The key to Mrs C's attitude to reminiscence lay in her amused and ironic reaction to finding herself among 'ordinary' people in a hospital ward. Her self-concept emphasized the social distance derived from her relatively prosperous early life and in particular her years as a local councillor. It was clearly a painful experience to realize that she had now become one of the 'old dears' whose facilities she had once inspected:

> All very smart to look at, as you went round the stairs – huge flowers in every room, but no comfort for the old dears. They got up in the morning – I went there several times, so I took a lot of notice – and they had the television on all day long, it never went off. They went to bed about eight o'clock, not disturbed or anything else, not allowed up until eight o'clock

in the morning – oh, I thought it was awful. Not awful to look at – the surface was very nice . . .

J.A.: Just a bad life?

Oh dear! I remember one old dear, I expect now she had cancer. I don't know how I got to know her – through one of the Councils, I expect, but she begged me to send her some pills. Would I take them out of the box? Because if they knew she had pills, they would take them away. She died very soon afterwards, and I expect it was cancer, but I've no proof of that. But the other is gospel truth. It was all there for show, but what good did it do?

Mrs C had been a member of the Labour Party all her life:

My father was a staunch Liberal, and I was Labour and it used to annoy him. He used to take the mickey and say, 'There goes Mo with her little red flag!' By the time I was about forty-something I began to be active. We had committee meetings on one, perhaps two, nights a week, from seven to half-past ten – it goes on and on. I was assistant secretary, then I was secretary – a busy bee! Well, not really and truly, but you gained experience and you got well known, and I have enjoyed it. When I became a councillor I was on the libraries committee, which of course is only natural, the way I read all the time. I was on three or four other committees, and I helped to run the clean food committee. Now I don't think it did very much, but it went round and poked its nose in!

From her position on the hospital ward, Mrs C tried to make sense of the steep decline in her fortunes. As we talked it became clear that she considered that the rot had set in during the Second World War. Her experience on the building committee which was responsible for repairing bomb damage in the borough was particularly significant. It seemed to her that the council's generosity was shamelessly exploited:

Oh, they managed to fit in somewhere, most of them, like pigs in pokes! They were not obviously hard up. They hadn't got cash, and hadn't got furniture or anything else, but I remember that they got blankets and things all given to them. Lots of them swung the lead – hate to say that, but it's true! – Trust me to put my foot in it!

J.A.: What, they claimed for more that they'd lost, and that sort of thing?

They claimed for as much as – if not more! They do now, don't they? I mean you and I know that. You don't shout about it and I shouldn't say it aloud!

Mrs C was adamant that things had been markedly different in her younger days, and that it was not simply the passing of time which made the past seem more attractive than the present:

The spirit of helping each other *was* better, and if anybody was in trouble you'd sort them out. I remember as a kid being sent to someone who lived opposite us. My mother sent me, and it appeared that they had got scarlet fever. I took some food over, but you wouldn't hear of anything like that now. See that's where it's all gone – you don't sort of bother. I used to know nearly everyone in my road, but not now because all the old dears like me have either gone to live with their kids, or gone in homes, or pegged out. Perhaps I know a couple – that's all. Funny how you don't know anymore. It's 'Blow you Jack, I'm OK!' Now is that from having too much money and too many good things?

In order to characterize the decline in standards and social attitudes which she had witnessed during her lifetime, Mrs C liked to invoke an earlier 'golden age'. Although her ascerbic observations on contemporary life were easy to follow, her account of this time was rambling and incoherent:

My father used to drive a couple of horses and a cart, course they didn't have cars – well he did have a car – and always drive in the middle of the road, because he'd always been in the middle of the road, hadn't he? And always a little bit windy, course nowadays a man is brought up in a car. I can remember particularly Greenwich – I used to go with him sometimes – I used to see from the top of the road to the hills. You could see the river down, and I remember it was Greenwich. Should you have that memory?

Discussion

While Mrs C's interview contained some narrative material, her concept of a 'golden age' in the past seems to fall into the category of escapist reminiscence. As Watt and Wong describe it, escapist reminiscence:

Takes on the tone of fantasy/daydreaming as the reminiscer dwells on the good old days as a means of escaping from a gloomy present. [It] often involves an exaggeration of past glories and devaluation of the present.

(Watt and Wong 1991:50)

The overt theme of Mrs C's account was that life had been better in the past, as expressed in the vague sayings about childhood or in her pride in her political career. However, she also recorded the comment that 'you don't *want* to remember, I think that's it. You push it aside, don't you.' Indeed, from time to time in the interview, Mrs C seemed unable to suppress hints that the 'good old days' might not have been quite as idyllic as she had tried to suggest. For example, on sex: 'you pick up any book, it tells you things I never knew. I wonder if I missed anything, I often do'; on working as a maid in a grand household: 'it opened your eyes to things, perhaps that's why I wanted different things'; and on changes in funeral customs: 'whether that is worse or better, I don't know.'

Conclusion

While the development of taxonomies for reminiscence represent an important step forward in understanding rich and diverse phenomena, it remains to be seen how successful such attempts at classification will ultimately be. As reminiscence presents nurses and others with the opportunity to listen to the patient as an individual, it seems rather illogical to pigeon-hole that individuality into a predetermined category which is held to 'explain' that patient. Yet there are powerful professional and institutional pressures encouraging the development of just such universal systems, so that a uniform practice of reminiscence may be established. Taxonomies are helpful in reminding us that there are many different types of reminiscence, and that some approaches may be more adaptive than others, but they should not be allowed to take the place of an individual response to a personal life-history. The work of Helen Evers (1981) has helped to illuminate the world of the long-stay geriatric ward, and she has offered 'stereotypes' to illuminate the experiences of women patients. However, these were the views of an observer looking in from the outside, while reminiscence offers us the patient's own perspective expressed in her own words.

By listening again to these tape-recordings made in the clinical environment, I have been forced to realize how little I had taken in during the actual interviews. My questions were often irrelevant and disrupted the flow of the discourse, or simply demanded information that had already been given. Returning to these interviews has helped to bring home to me the richness of reminiscence and the importance of developing the skills to hear what is really being said. The interval of several years which has elapsed between the making of the recordings and my review of them has enabled me to make constructive use of recent concepts. This has given me a new appreciation of the power and complexity of reminiscence which I am bringing to my current work in the field.

_8_

'I got put away': Group-based reminiscence with people with learning difficulties

_____ DOROTHY ATKINSON _____

Introduction

'This is the first time anything I have said has been written down.' These words spoken by Doreen Cocklin, were included in an anthology of prose, poetry and art by people with learning difficulties: _Know Me As I Am_ (Atkinson and Williams 1990:168). This spoken-but-written sentence introduced a short statement by the author about herself, and the written form was obviously of importance to her. Indeed, the anthology itself, as a published collection of (often oral) accounts of the lives of people with learning difficulties, has been the source of pride and celebration for its many contributors.

The project described in this chapter has built on some of my earlier work as co-editor of the anthology. Although much smaller and more focused, in terms of scale and numbers, my recent project – a series of group-based reminiscence sessions with nine older people with learning difficulties – also resulted in a written product, again one which was highly prized by its contributors. This chapter, therefore, not only looks at the _process_ of constructing and reconstructing individual and collective memories, it also considers the value to its members of the _product_ of the group's work; a written booklet entitled _Past Times_ (Atkinson 1991).

The 'history group' – as it was known to its members – was distinctive in its use of reminiscence in two ways. First, it involved _people with learning difficulties,_ people who – even in recent publications which chart history 'from below', including accounts by working-class people, women and members of minority ethnic groups – remain largely excluded and 'invisible' (Bornat 1992). Second its reminiscence work led to the production of a _written_ account of an individual and shared past.

Membership of the group was determined by a process of informal intro-
ductions and meetings, and a personal invitation to potential members to
take part in a series of group discussions about past events and personal
experiences. In inviting people to join the group, I had two research aims in
mind. One aim was to collect narrative accounts of people's lives against the
background of key legislative and policy changes in the learning disability
field in this century; to co-construct a history 'from below' (Humphries
1984:x). A second and interlinked aim was to find the ways and means of
doing this; to test a *method*. Could a group of people with learning difficulties
use recall and reminiscence to produce oral accounts of their past lives?

As the method did, in fact, prove viable, and rich accounts were told and
recorded on tape, a third and shared research aim emerged; that these accounts be transformed into a written oral historical account of the group
members' lives and experiences. The written format was important to the
group members. Although most people were unable to read well or fluently
(if at all), nevertheless they saw the written word as authoritative; somehow
their spoken memories were validated by being written down. Earlier drafts
of this written account later acted as 'trigger' materials and fed into a continuing process of recall and reminiscence. Thus a series of readings of earlier
versions of 'our book' (as it became known) led to the revealing of hitherto
hidden layers of memories; these more 'private' accounts built on and added
to the earlier 'public' accounts (Cornwell 1984), and helped determine the
shape, structure and content of the final product, *Past Times*.

Background to the project

The anthology, *Know Me As I Am*, helped set the scene for the research project
in two ways. It had demonstrated in numerous ways and formats the 'richness, depth and diversity of people's memories', and had suggested that,
'Much social history, particularly of long-stay hospitals, still remains to be
told from "below" and "within" (Atkinson and Williams 1990:243).
Although most contributions had been from individuals, a significant number
were from groups (e.g the Women's Group and the Experiences of Handicap
Group). While many individual accounts were told in rich detail and depth,
the group accounts incorporated commonalities and differences, shared insights and glimpses of a hidden world; thus echoing points made by Paul
Thompson (1988) in his discussion of the use of groups in life-history work.
The challenge, as I saw it, was to aim for the richness of detail and depth,
captured in individual accounts, but within the more insightful and reflective
mode of a group setting.

The use of recall and reminiscence with older people generally has been
well documented over the years (recent examples include Coleman 1986;
Bornat 1989; Gibson 1989; and Fielden 1990). However, documented accounts of the use of similar approaches with older people with learning
difficulties are still very rare. One example is the work of Potts and Fido
(1991), which documents the history of a long-stay institution through the
reminiscences of seventeen of its older current and ex-residents. Their project
was based on interviews, rather than group-based reminiscence, but they also

included readings of their work as a means of feeding back to participants on the product-in-the-making.

The group

The group consisted of nine people, seven men and two women. Their age range was 57–77 years, with most people in their late sixties or early seventies. I made contact with potential members via 'special' services, which meant that the membership was drawn entirely from residential and day-care settings. In the event, they had two things in common: they all currently lived in the same county (and, with two exceptions, had always lived there), and (with only one exception) they had spent much of their lives in long-stay hospitals. The county address proved a tenuous link in practice, as in their earlier days, they had lived in different villages and towns. The hospital link was important, however, and led to the sharing of many memories of institutional life.

The project spanned most of two years, though it was never intended (by me) to last so long. Despite my many and persistent doubts along the way, the weekly – and later fortnightly – group meeting soon became a popular event in the members' lives. The group had an extended existence because it provided a forum where experiences could be remembered, re-lived and shared. The group members had an opportunity to recall, and reflect on, much of their past lives, and to begin to make sense of some of their experiences. In addition, the group format made possible the sparking off of individual and shared memories between members.

The process

It was difficult, at the time, to spot overall trends or directions in the development of the group. Most of my attention, in group meetings, was focused on trying to hear and understand the confidences, the exchanges and the messages of the moment. It is only in retrospect that I can see the unfolding history of the group. In reconstructing that history, I can now identify four phases, each one triggered off – albeit unwittingly – by a change of direction on my part. These phases are as follows:

Phase 1: 'Public' accounts;
Phase 2: Period details;
Phase 3: 'Private' accounts;
Phase 4: A collective account.

Although identifiable now, these phases were not distinct or separate; rather, they were interlinked and overlapping. Thus, some 'public' accounts, which characterized phase 1, in fact recurred at intervals throughout the group's life; and the same could be said for the other types of accounts. Thus each phase represents an *overall* trend or direction in the nature and content of discussions, not a clearly bounded episode. As such, they are useful devices for enabling me to reconstruct the group's life. I will now take each phase in turn; they are in chronological order. In order to illustrate the workings of the group *at the time*, the extracts in the following sub-sections are taken directly from tape transcripts.

Phase 1: 'Public' accounts

In the early days of the group, my intention was to introduce shared themes, of a universal kind, for people to respond to. The rationale for this was that, in its formative stages at least, it was important for the group to have relatively non-threatening topics to focus on. My initial list of themes thus included memories of childhood and adolescence in terms of where (type of house and neighbourhood), how (home and community life) and with whom (family life and relationships) group members lived. Discussion of hospital life in particular, was left until later in the group's evolutionary cycle.

The group meetings lasted for an hour and, with permission, were tape-recorded. I was accompanied at each session by one or two staff members from the residential or day settings who knew at least some of the participants well. (Staff helped in numerous ways: they organized transport; offered reassurance and support; joined in with their own memories; and helped interpret and translate people's responses.)

This initial phase was characterized by group members speaking, on the whole, directly to me and recalling their individual and 'public' memories. Although these memories, to my surprise, included references to traumatic events, they were shared with remarkable readiness. There were, however, as I found later, other more private stories behind these public statements. The distinction I am making here is between the rehearsed account, that is one that has been told and re-told over time and is readily shared, and the more personally revealing and unrehearsed accounts of the past (what I call here private accounts). Although the former may (and in practice did) include mention of what must have been painful or tragic happenings in people's lives, that pain had, it seemed, receded through a process of telling and re-telling over time. The later unrehearsed accounts (the private accounts) still had the capacity to conjure up, and convey to others, the remembered pain.

The following extract is taken from the tape transcript of what was only our second meeting. It features a revealing exchange between myself ('D') and 'Enid' (no real names are used in this account):

> *E:* And then, of course, I was put away because of my father, because he was no good. I got put in a children's home.
>
> *D:* Your father was no good?
>
> *E:* Yes. When I was a little baby, I got put away.
>
> *D:* [quietly] Oh, I see.
>
> *E:* He was no good.
>
> *D:* That's sad. What was wrong with your dad?
>
> *E:* Well, he used to go out drinking every night and, erm, he used to hit my mother.

Phase 2: Period details

From the outset, I was concerned about how to keep the group going and how to maintain people's interest. As we – rather rapidly, I thought – worked through my list of themes in the early meetings my anxiety grew that we (or I) would soon need some external input to stimulate discussion. This led to my recourse to reminiscence tapes, slides, photographs, cigarette cards and other period items; thereby, as it turned out, ushering in phase 2 of the group's life. (Although, in retrospect, the early memories evoked by my themes were often full, rich and revealing, as the above extract demonstrated. The unease was entirely mine.)

The reminiscence aids were greatly enjoyed. They helped bring out the commonalities between people's experiences. We could all (this includes myself and staff as well as the group members) join in with our own memories of mangles and marbles. Furthermore, the various aids helped the group members relate more directly to each other, as one person's memory inevitably sparked off somebody else's. This phase was characterized by the sharing of memories which led to the capturing of some period details. The following extract is an exchange triggered off by a picture of an early model of a vacuum cleaner; the participants are 'Godfrey', 'Barry' and 'Marjorie':

G: It's what you did the carpet with.
B: It's a vacuum cleaner, an old-fashioned one.
G: We didn't have one, we used a pan and brush. If we had to scrub the floor we used a bucket of water and a bit of soap. We used to scrub the floor on our hands and knees.
B: We had a bucket and mop.
M: We used a brush and pan. We scrubbed the kitchen floor.
G: [addressing staff] You younger generation, you don't do that today!

Phase 3: 'Private' accounts

At a later stage of the group's life, and in order to enable some of the quieter members to have a say, I introduced small-group work. This meant that we spent the best part of several sessions working in pairs or small groups of twos and threes (each pair/sub-group being accompanied by myself or one of the members of staff). This led, again, to the revealing of individual memories, but often of a deeper and more intensely personal kind.

These hitherto unrevealed, and unrehearsed, accounts still had the capacity to recreate some of the pain of the remembered experience. In a very real sense, the small groups or pairs enabled people to recall, relive and reflect on key events in their past lives. This engaged the group members in a process of life-review. It was only in such a sub-group, for example, that Godfrey revealed the hidden story of his early family life, as the following extract illustrates:

D: So your mother used to do the shopping?
G: Yeah, yeah.
D: In the village?
G: I think I was better off without her. She didn't like me, I don't know why. Me dad and me were just the opposite, I got on well with him.
D: And with your mother?
G: She used to hit me, knock me around. I used to come home from

school, and if anyone had come home with me, a little boy or a little girl, and we'd had a bit of fun, she'd say: 'I'll deal with you!'

Phase 4: A collective account

The fourth phase of the group's life was characterized by 'readings' from the group members' own work; the first, second and third drafts of the booklet, *Past Times*. I compiled the first draft from the tape transcripts of the first 15 meetings, and read the entire contents to the group over a period of weeks. The readings took a long time because the booklet acted as very personalized trigger material to the group members, and drew out more detailed accounts and further examples. The second and third drafts were produced in the same way, following the same sequence. It is likely that this process could have continued indefinitely, as each set of readings led to the revealing of more and more memories.

One key feature of this last phase was the emergence of shared memories of hospital life. Sometimes the mention, by one person, of specific names, or the recall of a particular incident, would spark off somebody else's memory of that time. An interesting feature of this phase, though, was that shared accounts could also emerge between people who had lived in different hospitals, or the same hospital at different times. The following example is of the 'sparking-off' variety; it involves Godfrey and Marjorie, who were in the same hospital at the same time:

> *M:* After 20 years we changed over, and it was Sister 'Smith'.
> *D:* Was she on the children's ward?
> *M:* She was on F2. And then we had 'Moffatt'. She was on F1. She died in the end.
> *G:* She was a wicked old devil, she was! No wonder she died!
> *M:* Old devil?
> *G:* Yes!
> *M:* You're telling me! And Smith!

While the group format, where memories were exchanged and shared, led to a consensus view of institutional life, it was a consensus of a particular kind. In a very real sense, it served to sustain and justify the group's distinctive history, a history which hitherto has largely remained hidden or marginalized.

The product

In the earlier phases of the group's life, my emphasis was on the 'normal' life-course. Thus reminiscence was directed, first, by my themes of childhood, home life, schooldays and so on and, later, by reminiscence aids which emphasized shared experiences and commonalities between people, and which led to some sharing of period details. Thus my starting point was with 'normal' life and 'typical' experiences, and was an attempt to draw out those memories which group members had in common with other people, rather than dwelling on their differences.

This approach worked in the sense that many individual and shared memories emerged of rural and urban working-class life in the early and middle years of this century. There was apparent enjoyment in being able to recall, and share with everyone else (including myself and staff), rich details of the bathtimes and washing days of childhood. 'Barry', for example, recalls the family washday in the following extract:

> We did our washing down the cellar. We used to have a stone sink down there. We used to have an old mangle machine, and a tub for your clothes. We used to poss 'em in, peg 'em up. We used to put a line across the street and hang our clothes out.

However, the members of the group had, on the whole, led far from 'normal' lives and consequently had not enjoyed many of life's 'typical' experiences. They were single and childless; they had, with one exception, lived for extended periods in institutions, and had spent much of their lives excluded from paid employment. Thus they had individual and collective memories which were very different from the experiences of most people of their age and class. I will illustrate this marked – and articulated – different-ness with examples of both individual and shared memories; this time the extracts are taken from the final draft of *Past Times*. On the whole, the group members were aware of how their lives differed from other people's so that even a celebratory tale of a remembered achievement, such as getting a job, was likely to contain a cautionary note about how it ended with the sack.

Individual memories

Every group member, at some point, revealed painful memories from childhood. Often these were around the themes of loss, separation or rejection. Enid, as we saw earlier, was taken into care as a baby; 'Jim', in the following extract, remembers the last time he saw his mother:

> I never had a dad. I was at 'Peartree' in Cambridge, it was a home and school. I was eight. That was the last time I saw my mum. She used to write to me, the staff read them to me, the letters. My mum lived in Bedford by the river, in a home. I think she died in 1971. I didn't want to go to the funeral.

By way of contrast, 'Barry' lived with his parents until well into his adult life. He attended the local school; though, as the following extract illustrates, this was at some cost to himself:

> I used to wear a dunce's hat. She used to put a big cap on my head and it said on the front 'Dunce'. 'Cos I couldn't write.

Shared memories

The loss of home, family and freedom, which long-term hospitalization brought about, were remembered and felt keenly. These memories were, of course, very personal ones. But other memories were evoked of hospital days which, at least in the telling, were characterized by defiance and humour. The tales of hospital life often contained a role-reversal – the patient became the 'hero', and the charge nurse, doctor or superintendent was portrayed as the 'fool'. In the following example of the genre, narrated by 'Godfrey', his co-conspirators are 'Arthur' and 'Fred' and the object of their attention on this occasion is 'Baxter', the farm bailiff employed by 'Talltrees' Hospital:

> Baxter was the farm bailiff when we were at Talltrees, and he had a bike. Me and Fred, and old Arthur, we used to get together and put it up the chimney. There used to be a, you know, those big chimney pots on top of those farmhouses. We had a big rope, and we tied old Baxter's bike on this rope and put it right up the chimney. And of course, this certain afternoon, Arthur had done it. It was a Friday, and old Baxter comes out of his office and says: 'Goodnight you men, I'll see you on Monday, it's my weekend off'. 'Course, old Baxter couldn't find his bike, he didn't know where it was.

Conclusion

One of the interesting findings to emerge from this study was the value to people with learning difficulties of the reminiscence process itself. While this was intended to be a research project to chart the lives and experiences of group members, and to find the ways and means of doing so, it had other unintended and beneficial consequences. Reminiscence, it seemed, could lead to an enhanced sense of self and greater self-esteem. In this project, the combined effect of both the *process* of group-based reminiscence – which was, it seemed, intrinsically enjoyable for the participants – and the emerging/evolving *product* (*Past Times* in its various manifestations), served to bring about a sense of individual achievement and a collective pride. Thus the project makes at least some contribution to the reclaiming of personal pasts, and in that sense played a part in enabling hitherto unspoken/unheard voices to emerge.

Similarly, the project also makes a contribution to the reconstruction of the 'hidden history' of hospital life, and towards the reclaiming of a shared or collective past. This project was in itself only a modest venture into the use of reminiscence with people with learning difficulties, and clearly much more remains to be done. However, the project at least demonstrates that the approach has the potential to enable people to look back on their lives and remember past events, to develop an awareness of an unfolding individual history, and to reflect on the meaning of individual and collective experience.

The written account, *Past Times*, remains an important outcome of the group's work. It may seem ironic that people who, for whatever reasons, are excluded from access to the written word, still value it so highly. Yet it is that very exclusion which makes a written account so necessary – for such an account has a sense of permanence (compared with oral accounts) and enables people with learning difficulties to communicate their experiences to others. Thus memories are validated, a sense of continuity is established and maintained, and people 'speak' with an authoritative voice.

Reminiscence in itself is valuable, but the written word – especially for people with limited access to or input into documented history – is potentially powerful. The combination is a potent mix. It enables hitherto 'invisible' people to be seen at last.

Acknowledgements

I wish to thank all the people who took part in this project for their generous investment of time, energy and enthusiasm. This includes the group members themselves and the staff who worked alongside them.

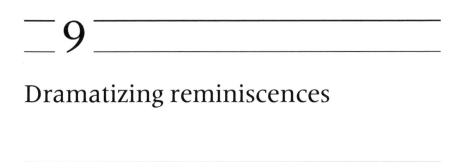

9

Dramatizing reminiscences

___ PAM SCHWEITZER ___

First steps in reminiscence

I first realized the effectiveness of reminiscence in 1982, while working as an education officer for a community organization working with pensioners in South East London.[1] My previous experience had been ten years in the fields of educational drama in schools and of professional theatre in educational contexts. I had thought that I would be leaving all that behind when I began working with older people, but in practice the two worlds have fused in a natural and highly productive manner, leading to new creative approaches to reminiscence and a new form of theatre basing itself on older people's memories.

Using the Help the Aged *Recall* pack of tapes and slides, I held a series of reminiscence sessions in sheltered housing units in Greenwich. I watched people who had been reluctant to attend the group because they were shy or felt they had nothing to contribute, take themselves and everyone else by surprise. Memories flowed as a result of the sounds and images of the *Recall* pack, and people were triggering each other's memories with vivid recollections of local incidents.

As the stories emerged, I felt privileged to be the sole listener, apart from the participants themselves, and I felt they deserved a much wider audience.[2] It seemed important to record these stories in some way and to make them available to younger generations. As an education officer, I had been looking for more fruitful liaisons between children and older people than the rather old-fashioned, charity-based volunteer work which children in the area were doing at that time. Much of this work tended to reinforce their view of older people as helpless and needy. I was anxious to present the children with the more positive and vigorous view of older people that I was seeing. They were wonderful storytellers. They could make the past come alive. Their energies and competence appeared to increase as they recalled their own more active days when they ran a large family on a tight budget, or cut a fine figure at a local dance, or performed a skilful job.

So the older people agreed to reminisce with children in schools. They would visit local primary schools and talk about their own school days, or visit the local comprehensive school and talk about their experience of home economy in the 1920s. Those who were too physically frail to go out, agreed to meet sixth-formers from the local schools in the lounge and talk with them about aspects of their own younger days.[3] Many positive inter-generational contacts came out of this programme, but one method shone out above the rest as creating good relationships between old and young, and that was working together through drama.

Educational drama and reminiscence

Perhaps because my own experience as a teacher lay mainly in the world of drama, it was through that medium especially that I felt competent to bring young and old together. To give just one example among many from this period, a small group of sixth-form students from a local girls' school wanted to make a play as part of their 'A' level Theatre Studies course about what life had been like for young women of their own age (16–17 years old) in the 1920s, so arrangements were made for them to visit one of the sheltered housing units which had been having reminiscence sessions. Six women in their late seventies and early eighties agreed to meet the school students on a weekly basis to help with their project. At the end of the period, the resulting play was performed for all the residents in the unit. The girls needed to think about aspects of their own lives which were important to them, in order to work out what questions to ask the older women. They knew they would need to have plenty of detailed information and be able to remember it all if the scenes they were going to make were to feel real, so they armed themselves with tape-recorders and worked out a questionnaire. How did girls talk to their mothers or their boyfriends and what kind of music and dancing was popular? What would they have worn and who would have paid for it? How would they spend their spare time? Were they still at school, and if not, what kind of jobs did they do and how much did they get paid?

The special quality of the contact grew out of the students' need to listen with particular attention to the older people in order to create their own dramatized versions of what they had heard. They could not just write notes on what they heard and reproduce the facts. They had to find out about the feelings behind the facts in order to be able to identify with, to become, the older people in their young days. They had to work on the stories creatively and empathetically, bringing into their improvisations their own experience of life and relationships. They had to find ways of bringing the stories together to make something new out of them; a story with characters, with humour and with action. The older people could see that the girls valued what they had to tell and genuinely needed all the information they could supply. They watched the development of the play with interest, and they felt that they had a stake in its success. It was very much a joint project, and a special relationship based on mutual respect developed through working together creatively.

When the piece was performed for all the residents, it was warmly received.

The rest of the audience, about thirty residents, immediately identified with the material, laughing with recognition at the play where it felt right, and anxious to correct where it felt wrong. The performance led naturally to a great deal of animated reminiscence at the party which followed. A small number of people, old and young, had created the piece, but many more had responded to it in performance, and I saw that the technique had the potential to reach a still wider audience.

Establishing the Age Exchange Reminiscence Theatre Company

It was the experience of a number of projects of this kind involving young and old people working together making plays from memories which encouraged me to set up the Age Exchange Theatre in 1983, as a professional production company dedicated to reminiscence theatre. The two great merits of using professionals were that they would be able to create theatre of a high standard for an audience which was noticeably under-served but particularly responsive, and that they would be able to tour it far more widely than the school pupils had been able to manage. However, it seemed very important to hang on to the key stages by which these early plays had been put together and presented. That is, the choice of a broad reminiscence theme which has a wide appeal to older people and a particular interest to those creating it; an agreement to a joint working relationship with older people in which their stories would determine the content of the play; the tape-recording of memories and the careful attention to those recordings; the involvement of the older people in the emerging drama; the recognition of their role as experts; the presentation of a play in their space; and the post-performance discussion involving the whole audience.

For our first show, 'The Fifty Years Ago Show', we invited older people in four sheltered housing units to reminisce on the theme of the effect of the Depression on family life in the early 1930s. The unemployment figure of three million recorded in 1933 had just been reached again in 1983, lending the show considerable topical interest. We explained to the older people involved that we would have to find a dramatic framework which would carry their memories effectively to other audiences. This would involve selecting and editing in order to create a plot and a set of characters who were both individual and representative, and with whom our audiences could identify. By contrast with the previous school projects, where the process of dramatizing memories and the product – the performance – had both taken place on home ground, the advent of a professional touring company would entail a certain loss of control of their material, but with the considerable advantage that it would be reaching a far wider audience, and hopefully stimulating further reminiscence.

Improvising around the memories

Skilful improvisation by actors around the stories given to us proved to be the most effective way of triggering more detailed recollections. Through emotional involvement with the characters created by the actors, the older people were transported back into an earlier reality, remembering a great deal more about the feelings engendered by those events in the process. I remember one woman whose story we were planning to present in an improvised form, saying that she felt rather low and would not be attending the session. She was prevailed upon to come when she heard that it was her own story which the actors had been working on, and on which they sought further comment. Once the process was under way, she told a great many more stories about the tailoring workshop in which she had worked and the people she remembered. She advised on wages, tailoring processes, numbers of items to be turned out in a single day, working hours and safety regulations, stressful disputes with management, her own personal anxiety about failure to keep pace with the demands of the work, her friends at work who kept her going, and the impact of her wages on the family. She was the focus of everyone's attention, and the satisfaction of seeing her new input immediately put to use visibly lifted her depression.

Some of the older people participated actively in the improvisations. Initially, they commented from their chairs on the actors' interpretations, suggesting lines of action or things which might be said. Then, given the opportunity, some of them were willing to get up and show how it should be done, replacing one or more of the actors in the improvisations. Ostensibly, they were willing to do this in the interests of helping the actors to achieve greater accuracy, but the process of playing out the past was clearly an invigorating one, and one which came quite naturally.[4] The actors' ability to sustain the illusion, by responding appropriately in their roles to leads from the older people, helped them to suspend disbelief further.

I had no doubt that those involved altered their perceptions of themselves and each other (even if only for a little while) as a result of this activity. A woman who was often withdrawn and depressed was interviewed after the experience of joining in such an improvisation, and she said, 'I'll do anything. If anybody asks me, I will. I'll do anything.' And I am sure she did feel at that moment that anything was possible because of the new confidence the experience of successfully dramatizing had given her. Even though the improvisation was about a difficult situation which she had experienced, an altercation with the Relieving Officer and a family row about whether the father had been foolish to show him the door, playing it out had lifted her spirits. She had seen that by making her own history public in the improvis-ation, it had been transformed into something more like social history, part of a pattern of common experience which made sense in time. It had not lost any of its sharp personal detail by having been incorporated into the larger picture.

When it came to deciding what stories should be included in the play, one rule we adopted was that if a story cropped up a great many times in different forms, it should have a place. It would obviously reverberate across diverse audiences, and would be likely to give rise to many memories. Since the generation of reminiscence was one of our objectives in touring, we ear-marked certain stories and took the liveliest versions, or even combined different but related experiences.

Another question which arose early in our devising period was what we should do with the reminiscences which we had collected and transcribed, but which we could not find a place for in the eventual play. We realized that the memories we had collected offered a window on to a period which was of interest to an enormous number of people, young as well as old, and that it would be somehow wasteful not to preserve these stories, beyond the lifetimes of the narrators. So we decided to go into print with the memories and to illustrate them with the hundreds of photographs which the older people had brought to the reminiscence sessions to help the actors with their research. Ever since the first Age Exchange show, this has been a pattern, and the books of memories accompanying the shows have given the whole reminiscence theatre process a permanence which it would otherwise have lacked.[5]

On the road with reminiscence theatre

Playing to seven audiences a week in widely differing venues, the theatre company soon got used to widely differing responses to the performance. In some venues, they would be given a royal reception by audiences who were so in tune with the play that they were speaking the lines almost before the actors. Everyone would be singing along as popular songs of the 1930s pointed up the emotional or humorous moments of the play. People would spontaneously offer words of comfort and identification with the characters. There was one occasion when an audience member, whose stories had been included, identified so strongly with the material that she stood up on the front row and turning to the rest of the audience announced, 'This is my show. It all comes from me.' More often though, people would come up to the actors afterwards with tears in their eyes and say, 'You told my story this afternoon. I don't know how you could have, because you're much too young to know about it, but that was my life.' The cathartic effect of the shows, and the resulting reminiscences in all kinds of settings where we played, were very satisfying for the company. Where care staff were also present at the shows, which was not always as often as we would have wished, the play was often a starter for them to run their own reminiscence sessions, and many responded to the opportunity we had created for these to occur.

At the other extreme, the actors might play to half a dozen people while fifty played bingo in the next room refusing to respond to the invitation to attend the play on the assumption that it would probably not be good, that they did not like theatre and that they did not wish to remember the grim 1930s, even assuming a bunch of fairly young actors (aged 22–40 years) could succeed in evoking them. Such responses were extremely rare, but we did encounter them, and it was difficult for the actors to cope with that sort of rejection. It certainly did take some time for the kind of work we were offering to find acceptance in some circles, and for people to realize that they could expect a high standard of entertainment. Since those beginnings in 1983, Age Exchange has reached hundreds of thousands of older people all over London and way beyond. We have created three or four touring shows each year, employing either improvisation methods to devise a script or, more frequently, a 'verbatim' method which we came to adopt.

Verbatim reminiscence theatre

Many of the older people whose memories we have recorded and transcribed during the research periods for the various shows had remembered events through dialogue in the form of direct speech, so their narrations were in a naturally dramatic form. The dialogue they remembered had a more authentic feel to it than anything the actors could create through improvisation. The contributors would hear their own highly individuated voices in the play, and they would speak directly to many others of a similar background and age group whose voices are not often heard. A group of actors working with me on a play about the Jewish East End, 'From Stepney Green to Golders Green', began the process by developing a series of powerful improvisations on which we intended to base the script. But they themselves were so moved by the intensity of the original versions or delighted by idiosyncratic, but wholly appropriate, turns of phrase, that we changed tack and created the text entirely from verbatim material. Often this involved telling part of a story direct to the audience as a memory before moving to enactment with other players. The following dialogue was given to us by the original storyteller remembering relatives crowding into the house at weekends:

> *Girl:* It was card playing amongst the grown ups. Solo.
> *Card playing woman:* So who didn't put in the kitty yet?
> *Card playing man:* By my life I put in already.
> *Woman:* Come on, come on. I'm sitting here like a golem with the ace and the jack in my hand.
> *Man:* Believe me, mein enemies should have such a partner. Next week, better you should go to the pictures instead.
> *Girl:* Mostly the women didn't play cards. I don't know what they did. Probably talked about marrying off their daughters. In the meantime, we children played in the street.
> *Song by all:* I give you a paper of pins.

The other great advantage of this approach was that the play text was not only in words the audience could readily identify with, but was also in a remembering mode ('We always used to. . .'), so that at the end of the play the transition to reminiscence was a very natural one.

Crossing cultural barriers

Where we work across language divides, using the verbatim method becomes more complicated. One important area of Age Exchange Theatre's work has been to build bridges between groups with very different experience and this can entail reflecting through theatre one group's experience to another. Working in a multicultural city like London, we have wanted to record and play the life-experience of many different minority groups of older people whose voices are not often heard. The text of these plays has mainly been in English, even where the original interviews were conducted in another language, but we have always included sections in the mother tongue, and the accompanying books have been printed in parallel bilingual text versions. These plays have obviously been of particular interest and value to the community whose histories they have portrayed and celebrated, but they have also afforded others some insight into the past lives and current concerns of older Jewish, Irish, Cypriot, Asian and Caribbean elders. However divergent the experience of the minority group, there is always identifiable common ground bringing different groups together through the human drama. An older Caribbean woman who saw our play 'Just Like the Country', based on the experience of older white Londoners who had been pioneers on the outer London cottage estates, commented: 'I felt lonely and isolated just like that when I first came to England.' When we took on tour to Germany a show based on older Punjabi people's memories of leaving India to settle in England, we were worried whether the audiences would connect with experiences we were portraying. In fact, older Germans who spoke neither English nor Punjabi were engaged by shared experience of youth, of financial hardship, of difficult decisions involving loss, of making a new life in a sometimes hostile environment, and of growing old away from childhood scenes and extended families. One older man in Cologne said, 'I didn't understand a word, but I understood everything.'

Active involvement of older people in rehearsals

Whether we are using the verbatim approach or arriving at a script through improvisation, the theatre company still always involves contributors in the rehearsal process. Sometimes they will improvise with us, or they will revise the text in rehearsal so that the dialogue sounds more authentic. They may suggest choreography which has a better period feel, or perhaps advise generally on the production. The actors, once they have got used to an initially rather daunting and invasive situation, find it very helpful to be given such powerful models. Some of the company's most effective scenes have been directed by their originators; for example, the Thames lightermen who came to rehearsals to teach the actors the art of handling a barge and the dockers who demonstrated how a two hundred-weight bag of sugar could be moved by one man. This is a time-consuming process for the theatre company, but it is also an effective way of reminding actors who may not have met the contributors during the research stage (since they are often working on a fully fledged script researched and written by someone else) of the particular nature of the work of Age Exchange; that they, as actors, are carrying the words and experiences of one group of people to another, and that it is important to 'get it right'.

In recent years, when we have been developing shows based on older people's memories for children at the Age Exchange Reminiscence Centre, we have even involved the contributors in the performances, alongside professional actors. The older people often have a part in the environmental design as well as in the performances, helping our professional designers on the scenery, costumes and props, sometimes contributing their own objects and, of course, their ideas about what it is vital to include.

Creating flexible models to meet different groups' needs

It was clear to Age Exchange from the beginning that there were more than enough audiences who could and did respond to our touring theatre shows in the way that we had hoped, but we did become aware that there was another kind of audience for whom what we were offering was not wholly appropriate. We were being asked to play in residential homes or long-stay hospital wards where audience members might sleep through whole scenes, or interrupt the show with comments which showed they were unclear about what we were doing in their space, or they might move around the room a great deal, or even occasionally shout abuse at the actors. When we discussed these incidents with staff afterwards, they usually urged us to continue coming to perform because there were people in the audience for whom the shows were a uniquely beneficial experience. They also assured us that even if we were a little thrown by some of the responses we encountered, they were impressed with the improvement in the concentration and involvement of their residents as a result of the performance.[6]

It remained open to question whether tightly structured hour-long reminiscence plays were the best option available. The actors sometimes had to assume a variety of roles, and maybe this added to the confusion. The story might jump forward in time, or move into a fantasy sequence, or be told from a different character's point of view, and an audience member who was teetering on the edge of sleep or dementia could hardly be expected to keep pace with all this.

In parallel to our touring theatre shows, we prepared a different kind of programme for these groups, something on a smaller scale, individually tailored to their needs, and more useful to the staff who were working with them. In 1986, we established the Age Exchange Reminiscence Project. We recruited and trained a group of arts workers from a range of backgrounds, all of whom had experience of working with groups and a desire to work with older people. We offered hospitals and homes an eight-session placement of two project workers to work with a small group of up to twelve residents or patients and to give support to the professional staff who were caring for them. At this time, there was a growing desire from health and social service workers for training in reminiscence, since its value was being more widely recognized. Over the years that this project has been operating, we have found that by working on their territory with their residents or patients, we can avoid the danger of unrealistic expectations of staff, and work with them to explore what is possible.

The Age Exchange Reminiscence Project

The arts workers prepare sessions involving a variety of arts activities around a reminiscence theme, and improvisation is one of these activities. For example, a session on shops and shopping might contain many of the following strategies, depending on the interest and ability of the group and the resources available. The workers collect together some objects connected with going shopping, such as a purse with old money in it, a string bag, some grocery items, Co-op tokens, a ration book, some sweets, butter hands, some weights.[7] These are passed around and each member of the group tells an associated memory, such as the time they were sent out by their mother to get something, but simply couldn't resist the temptation to buy something else, and then had to return and face the consequences. The group compiles a standard (period) shopping list and costs the items, considering where the earnings would come from to do this shopping. They discuss particular shops where they had credit, or which agreed to sell foods in very small amounts when times were hard. A small scene is then acted out by the Age Exchange workers in which a woman asks for credit and is refused. The group members are invited to take over these roles for a few moments, to show the workers how the negotiations went. The group recalls the local high street and what it looked like sixty years earlier. They list the various smells associated with it and with the local factories. Perhaps one of the project workers helps them to make a collage or a wall-plan or a three-dimensional mock-up of the high street, writing down everything the group remembers about the personalities who worked there or shopped there. The sounds of the high street are remembered, even represented by the group, and contrasted with what one might hear today. All these activities are undertaken by the whole group, including the staff, under the leadership of the project workers. The staff join in the sessions and gradually acquire the necessary skills and confidence to take over the running of the group.

The experience I referred to earlier of seeing older people in sheltered housing respond to invitations to participate in play-making and improvisation, convinced me that these approaches could work well in less obviously promising settings if the expectations were somewhat modified. In practice, we have found that drama exercises involving small pieces of role play by group members do have a special function in this sort of placement. They raise the energy level and physical confidence of the group, which is vital in settings where the main enemy is a creeping apathy.

Any reminiscence session can evoke painful memories, even where one would not have anticipated this from the theme under discussion, and dramatizing these painful memories can bring them into sharp focus. Of course, the same is true of painful memories evoked by our professional touring shows. We know that we will be stirring difficult memories, but the overall context in which they arise, as part of a broad canvas covering a range of experiences and emotions over time, can be a helpful way of giving them a different perspective. The process of working on these memories through drama in the small group context of the Reminiscence Project can sometimes allow the older person to re-experience them in a different context, and then let them go. Injustices seem to linger particularly long and remain very sharp in people's memories, and such stories can be played out in a way which helps to resolve the residual bitterness. The telling or enactment of these difficult memories can allow the older person to relive and then shed the painful memory, and move on with the rest of the group.

Small-scale enactments – one might almost describe them as short 'happenings' – provide an opportunity for individual older people to be the centre of attention, to be noticed. Whether they are showing how they used to flirt, demonstrating a work skill, acting out an angry confrontation with an employer, or performing a remembered party turn, they have the floor for a short while without feeling threatened by the exposure. Other members of the group will often applaud these animations and they will feel that something special has happened. The session itself becomes more memorable, and that can be very important in a context where memory of day-to-day events can be hard to maintain. When the group meets the next time, a short recap will bring the events of the last session back to mind in a pleasurable way and set up expectations of enjoyment for the present and future sessions.

Conclusion

Common to all the reminiscence theatre and drama work of Age Exchange, is the desire to value and celebrate the remembered experience of older people and to improve the quality of their lives in the present. Ten years after the first experiments in dramatizing memories, new approaches are emerging all the time. For example, some of the older people who have worked with us on projects over the years, are now performing their own memories. We are also evolving ways of performing our work for audiences in other countries, using mime and integrating more than one language into the script, since there is a great deal of interest internationally in the concept of reminiscence theatre as practised by Age Exchange.

Our most difficult task is to maintain the professionalism of our theatre and project work, while at the same time demystifying the reminiscence process and encouraging those with no previous experience to become involved.[8] The Reminiscence Centre which we created as our base in 1987 provides an invaluable meeting place for the professional arm and the grass-roots projects of Age Exchange. There, older people, actors, children, nurses, care staff and teachers encounter each other on an equal footing with a common interest in working creatively through reminiscence. There is far more general recognition of the value of reminiscence activity now than when I first encountered it in 1982, and Age Exchange has enjoyed the benefits of being part of a wider movement, which is gathering momentum all the time and increasingly crossing national frontiers. Like most people who have happened upon reminiscence, I feel that the past has a very promising future.

Notes

1 Task Force, a London-wide voluntary organization working with pensioners, later changing its name to Pensioners Link.
2 With one notable exception, the wardens of the sheltered housing units were not often willing to stay in the room for these sessions. They did not feel it was important for them to hear the memories of their tenants. I felt this was a great pity as the possibilities of one-to-one follow-up from the sessions in day-to-day life were wasted. It will be seen from what I describe later in the chapter that staff involvement seemed to me a high priority.
3 Many of these early experiments in reminiscence work across the generations are still in operation through the Age Exchange Reminiscence Centre in Blackheath, South East London, established in 1987.
4 Improvisation by older people around their own memories and the development in this manner of short plays for semi-public performance by the older people is now being further developed at the Age Exchange Reminiscence Centre. A group of people in their seventies called The Good Companions have also performed in shows with the children from the Age Exchange Youth Theatre, and more work along these lines is planned.
5 The books are also a valuable way of recording memories of minority groups of older people, and Age Exchange has published collections featuring Irish pensioners (*Across the Irish Sea*), Asian and Caribbean pensioners (*A Place To Stay* and *Remedies and Recipes*), with a book of Jewish older people's memories still pending. The books have been widely used by schools exploring the history of their local community, as well as by community groups themselves.

6 Staff in many venues got back in touch with Age Exchange after the performances, seeking support with running reminiscence sessions, and in most cases we were able to give some help, but it was only later that we put this support on a formal basis, offering staff training at our Reminiscence Centre and arranging Age Exchange placements in their own units.

7 Age Exchange has found that having objects to handle is such an effective reminiscence trigger in what often tend to be rather sterile environments, that we have produced a series of thematic collections of small items with creative ideas for how to use them with reminiscence groups. These Reminiscence Boxes are now mailed out all over the country.

8 *The Reminiscence Handbook*, by Caroline Osborn (published by Age Exchange 1993) is designed to address this need.

10

Turning talking into writing

_____ PATRICIA DUFFIN _____

Introduction

Perhaps one of the most significant outcomes of the last ten years of reminiscence work has been the value that has come to be given to the memories of ordinary people. This has not come about easily and undoubtedly there will continue to be those people who perceive reminiscence groups as little more than another way of filling-in time. However, the stream of published work, both from groups themselves as well as by those who act as facilitators, speaks very powerfully of people engaging afresh with their lives. While some groups may well remain at the talking to each other stage, for many others reminiscence has led to taping, writing, editing, publishing and performing something of their lives for others. The groups that have done this include very active as well as frail older people from both urban and rural settings. In the early days, there was certainly a predominance of white groups, but this has begun to change. Their commonality lies in telling their stories in their own words, not through the voices of others. Of course, this is how one expects the autobiographies of the rich and famous to be produced and it is the excitement of seeing ordinary people being able to do the very same thing that makes any involvement with reminiscence work so powerful and rewarding.

Most notable, perhaps, has been the use of group reminiscence. This has arisen directly out of reminiscence sessions where a number of older people have been meeting together over a period of time. In the early years of reminiscence work, this meeting was often seen as an end in itself. However, over time, it has become obvious just how important it is not only to hear those memories but also to try to find ways of storing them for posterity. In many cases, this has meant taping the sessions and using these as the basis for working towards writing. There are many routes that can be taken: writing during the group session; writing before or afterwards; writing at home;

writing in other groups with older people, including family. It is important for the facilitator to consider these possibilities and plan them into the life of the group. This is where having available other published reminiscences is so valuable. Again and again, in very different groups, I have seen just how significant it can be to see one's own experience matched in print by others. Rather than feeling in any way replicated, it can touch a chord that releases for people a sense of strength about what they have to say. It can enable them to recognize the value that others have placed on similar life-experiences. At the same time, it can act as a trigger whereby they are inspired to expand, match or disagree with those other lives. It can be a short step from this to considering the possibility of their own memories appearing in print.

In this chapter, I look at some of the ways in which such writing has been released, making use of my own experience in a variety of writing groups. At the same time, I discuss the question of just how possible it is to shift the emphasis in reminiscence groups towards a more concentrated look at the past through the thinking and sifting that writing demands. In literacy groups, which is where the bulk of my experience lies, there is always plenty of talk but it takes place in the context of preparing to settle down and write. The talk is leading on to a period of considering just what to write and how to say it. By definition, this means also a period of reflection before and during the writing and then the opportunity to add to or change what has been written. I wanted to see whether a similar shift in emphasis could take place in reminiscence groups. This means considering ways of getting people writing and then going on to reflect on ways of developing this further.

The fear of writing

When I started to write this chapter, I wondered at what point I should come clean about the title – 'turning talking into writing'. This was what I set out to do when I walked into my very first reminiscence session. I certainly expected to meet difficulties and some reluctance to write, that's a very familiar context for any workshop that I run as part of my job at Gatehouse. The Gatehouse Project (now Gatehouse Books Ltd) was set up in 1977 as a response to the need of adults with reading and writing difficulties for appropriate reading material. In those early days, of what was then known as the adult literacy campaign, adults who had the courage to come forward and seek help would often end up working on children's reading books. It took the insight and energy of various individuals and organizations such as *Write First Time*[1] to begin to present a very exciting alternative to this way of working. The alternative was to use those adults' own experience and their own words to create new and relevant reading material. Gatehouse set itself up in Manchester with two primary aims: to publish and distribute nationally some of the writing already generated in local groups; and to continue stimulating and supporting this specific group of new writers.

As you can imagine, going into an adult basic education (ABE) group not only to talk about writing but to make it happen, often within the same session, is fraught with tension and difficulty. Yet, out of hundreds of workshops that Gatehouse has run, this magic has never failed to happen. Talking, sharing ideas for writing and minimalizing the technical task of writing by offering a tape-recorder or another hand to take dictation, have reduced the size of the task. The outcome has often been excited and addicted new writers. One of the most significant factors in such workshops is the opportunity provided to talk openly about the fear and humiliation involved in keeping their difficulties with reading and writing secret from others. It often seems that breaking down this barrier and providing people with the opportunity to match experiences and support each other, sweeps away with it some of the fear of the written word. So, new writers can be born out of the knowledge that they are on a journey together with others and that strength comes from taking the risk, first, to talk and then to write. I went into my first reminiscence workshop expecting no less to happen.

Writing in a reminiscence group

By coincidence, I began working with two quite different groups of older people at roughly the same time. This came about as a result of being approached to see whether our particular groupwork skills could be applied to these groups. There were different reasons behind the two requests. The focus for the hospital group, which I describe first, was to encourage people to become less institutionalized and to develop a stronger sense of themselves as individuals. For the second group, residents of a sheltered housing block, the request was based on their own interest in the past and a curiosity about where that interest might go if someone came in to work with them on it.

The first group comprised female residents on a hospital ward and so they are described as frail older people. Most of them were there having come in initially because of a fall or an illness, but were then judged no longer to be able to look after themselves. So, they stayed on the ward while relatives tried to work out how to cope, or, having no relatives, they waited for alternative living space to be found. The more able, those who didn't need toileting and could still get around, stood a much higher chance of finding a place outside. The more needy and physically dependent had a much longer wait for too few places and so could end up living on the ward for a long time. So, potential group members could range from quite fit and alert women who were in for a short time, through to more institutionalized and therefore fairly inactive members. Women with dementia were not included in the group. We had discussed this at the beginning with hospital staff who felt that this would put too great a strain on the group. There was an idea that at a later stage we might have a small group consisting solely of patients with dementia to see whether this might spark off communication, but this never happened. However, the group regularly included women who were disorientated, confused or on medication that appeared to affect their ability to participate.

Two of us ran the group, myself and a writer with a community publishing background, Ailsa Cox. We began, as in any Gatehouse group, by encouraging the group to relax and talk to us and each other. In this way, everyone has a chance to contribute and to see that what they have to say will be taken seriously. By this stage, I had already revised my expectations of moving quickly into writing, both because I could see how physically frail most of the group were and also how difficult it was for them to maintain concentration. So, I decided to rely more heavily on taping group discussions to begin with.

Then, perhaps later, we could move on to encourage some of the women to write. I still expected to identify the difficulties that might prevent them from writing initially and to find ways of removing them. This whole period of work, which stretched over two years, was quite a special learning experience for me. Although a skilled group facilitator in the outside world, I had to accept very quickly that I had a lot to learn about these particular circumstances. With the help of staff at the hospital, I learned about how to make quite clear what I was offering. In Gatehouse groups, we work very much as facilitators: helping people to take control of their writing; being writers ourselves within the groups; playing down the organizing role as much as possible. So, we ran the early sessions very much in that style: informal, chatty, very little structuring, picking up comments from the previous week to develop and expand on. Part of what we were also doing here was sketching out for ourselves a wide, loose picture of the lives of the women in the group. This was to give ourselves a perspective to work from. Then we brought the tape-recorder into a session.

We explained that we wanted to tape the discussions as a way of holding on to their memories but also so that we could go back over them again together. In this way, we could add to stories and decide whether they had thought any differently about their memories since the previous meeting. In other words, we started to build a sense of development and continuity between meetings. After getting everyone's permission, we let the tape-recorder run for the whole session. Before the next workshop, we listened to the tape and wrote down the discussion just as it was said at the time. Our method was to listen to and transcribe the tapes ourselves. It would have been virtually impossible for someone who didn't know the group and hadn't attended the session to attach names to the voices. Also, because of the nature of the group, contributors might be talking all at the same time, or coming back in with contributions after the rest of the group had moved on. It was like putting together a jigsaw puzzle sometimes and it relied heavily on transcribing soon after the meeting so as to be able to recall events. We did decide to omit those parts of the session where the talk had gone completely away from reminiscence. We were fortunate to have help with the typing-up of these notes. Then we made enough copies for everyone and brought them back the following week. This was part of our plan to make something more permanent of the women's lives. However, it was at this stage we discovered that the group couldn't see the point of going on. Who would be interested, anyway? It wasn't until the transcripts of the typed discussion were passed around, that enlightenment came about. It was clear that everyone really relished seeing their words come back to them so quickly, and clearly. Heads nodded in agreement as the text was read back to the group. Soon, names were being corrected and more detail added. Finally, people clutched their copies to them and requested another copy to give to their family.

The change in the group's mood in such a short time was dramatic: from feeling confused and being controlled by others, their self-esteem had shot up to that of published writers. After initial disbelief that these sheets of typing could have anything to do with those sessions spent sitting and talking, they moved on quickly to pleasure and pride. As facilitators, we had brought in the transcripts as part of what we saw as an ongoing process of taping, reading the transcripts, working on them, then doing more taping. For us, it was very much a beginning. However, for the group, it was very different. They saw this as making sense of our meetings, at last. They had talked, we had taped and now they had their words back to read, to keep, to show their family. For those of us who have access, however difficult and limited, to ways of getting writing typed-up, it is quite a jolt to be reminded so strongly of what a privilege this is.

As a result of this, we set up much more structure when we began work on another ward. We produced a leaflet advertising the group and we worked out a ten week schedule focusing on themes and including visits from outside writers and groups. Always, we taped and transcribed. With the help of ward staff, we grew to know more about life on the ward and how it could affect one of our sessions. Obviously this is important because a night which has been disturbed because of illness, problems with medication, or a death, affects every member of the group next day. It is important to have this context in order to be able to respond to the changing needs or fears of the group. Sometimes this can involve altering your plan for the session, perhaps changing the emphasis to allow more opportunity for them to decide to use the session differently. As time went on, we became much more aware of fine changes taking place, for example, someone joining in for the very first time after a few weeks of saying nothing, and of the greater significance of this than in another group. We learned to cope with people forgetting who we were; deciding we were someone quite different; even crying at the sight of us. The role played by hospital staff here was crucial in helping us to gain some insight into this very different world that the women inhabited. It was the staff input which enabled us to bring in our experience of working in a variety of outside groups and to tailor it to the enclosed world of the hospital ward. In order to do this, we tried to learn to set aside our expectations and to respect the group's fragile links with the past.

At no point did anyone in the group ever write. For many, it would have been physically impossible. For others, we had to focus the session in order for them to maintain any sort of concentration. However, one woman who came in for a short while did give us a copy of her life story that she'd written at home before she joined the group:

> I, Jessie Jervis Pearson (Parker) was born 4th November 1894 in a three up and three down terraced house in 'The Sober Road', Mattram, Hyde, Cheshire. It was known by that name because of a plaque situated at the end of the road, which read as follows:
>> Be sober
>> Be industrious
>> Be economical.
>
> The house was owned by a family named Steel who owned most of the houses in the area. We paid a weekly rent, five shillings. We were lucky because we had a backyard and our own earth closet. We had a large open fireplace complete with oven. The water for washing was heated in a copper boiler. We bathed in a tin bath in front of the fire. When we grew up, we went to the public baths.
>
> Jessie Pearson
> (*Day In, Day Out*, included in Duffin 1992)

What we did with the group was arrange sessions around particular themes: childhood, work, the war. Each of these would have a variety of stimuli to get the talk started: photos; Gatehouse and Commonword[2] writers reading and talking; period clothes from the costume museum; trips, for example, to the Victorian street at Salford Museum; a video of local memories; music of the 1920s and 1930s.

Throughout all this we taped, transcribed and brought back typed copies of the discussions. This was done in order to keep the group constantly involved in remembering what they had talked about to give an opportunity to correct any errors made in transcribing and to change or elaborate on their memories. The next question was what to do with all of this material? We talked to patients and staff about whether they saw it being formed into a book or an exhibition. They decided on both!

Making writing public

So, we began the process of reading and sifting out what to use. This we did in the group – often sparking off more memories so that the material grew in depth. It was this that made us feel that we were producing a book that could be a good resource for other people.

Jessie: What else do I remember? Dolly tubs!

Josie: The wringing machine. A big wooden mangle. Nothing wanted ironing. And the lines in the streets. When anyone came up with the milk, you used to have to take the prop up.

Rose: You used to put your lines up and prop them up when it was a fine day out.

Ida: My brother caught his finger in the machine. My mother was turning a sheet and he put his hand down and he got his nail right off.

(*Day In, Day Out*, 1985:24)

Evelyn: Mother used to bake cakes, barm cakes o't Sunday, and sell them. Our Sam, he used to come in and she'd say, 'Where's them cakes gone?' Our Sam would've pinched two and took them out!

Ida: When my brother were at home, I used to make bread and biscuits. I used to do coconut buns and currant buns and fill them to t'top. As fast as they went in, they were out. I was lucky if I ever got one. Used to bring his mates in.

Monica: If you had a baking, every kid on the street had a butty. They used to dish them out, that's how poor they were, when they baked they'd give them all a butty. You all ate together.

(*Day In, Day Out*, included in Duffin 1992)

The culmination of all this was a launch in the hospital of the book and the exhibition. We tried to bring back as many women from the group as possible for this. There were over 150 people from the hospital, community education, residential homes, the press. There were readings from the book, some by the women themselves, others by older women writers from a Gatehouse writers' workshop. It was a celebration of the women's lives and a glimpse, for everyone else, of what took place during those hours spent talking and reminiscing.

A different reminiscence group

The second group that I was working with at this time was very different. They were residents of a sheltered housing block, all very active and independent, and leading busy lives. The first event I planned for this group was a visit from East Bowling History Workshop, Bradford. This group of pensioners began talking and writing together about their area and then went on to produce and sell their own books. They provided a very active demonstration of what I hoped to set up and ran a very lively session. However, once the new group began meeting there was lots of interest in reminiscence but strong resistance to the idea of writing. This was mainly because it was seen as a difficult thing to do and one woman said that she couldn't spell or write properly. What they did take to quite quickly was using the tape-recorder. A session spent with a group of half a dozen residents talking about work, school and games resulted in thirteen A4 typed sheets. Receiving these led to people bringing in their old photos to talk about, and be taped again.

This was a regular pattern, supplemented by trips out, including residents reading their transcripts to other groups. I tried to use the photos as a route into writing, encouraging people to jot down something about them, no matter how brief. There were lots of good resolutions but plenty of reasons given at the next meeting for why it wasn't possible. Sometimes I would work with a small group in a side room, but increasingly the other residents would want to get involved and quite often the discussion ranged around their large sitting-room, especially after a video or a new collection of photos had appeared. It was some fun trying to record any of this! In the end, it was one particular video, of a programme called 'Just like Coronation Street', that focused the group's memories. It sparked off a very animated discussion about the Blitz and anecdotes flowed thick and fast. My suggestion that these might be written-up got very little response. The idea of my bringing in the tape-recorder in order to do a 'special' was much more what people wanted, and that was what I did.

I began by reading excerpts from a similar discussion at the hospital workshop and then let the tape-recorder run on as the group talked steadily for three sides of tape. After checking through my transcript at the next meeting, they decided to use it as the basis of an exhibition to take place in the block on VE Day and to use this as the event they had been searching for in order to mark the anniversary of the sheltered housing unit itself. I provided a rough timetable of what needed to be done and when, and it just took off. We went to choose photos from Manchester Studies' archive at the then Polytechnic. The exhibition was called 'Where were you in the Blitz? Joseph Dean Court remembers the war years'. It consisted of ten very large panels (A1), each with photos and quotes from the taped discussion. These were divided up into a number of topics: shelters; evacuation; the blackout; rationing; bombing; women at work; making-do; VE Day. Then a completely unplanned element crept in as the residents dug up national registration cards, medals, flat-irons, newspaper clippings and gramophone records. These all went on display. A new panel was created from enlargements of people's childhood photos and provided a lot of fun on the day as people were encouraged to spot who they were. By the day itself, half the local area seemed to have been swept in. The residents acted as hosts, took people round the exhibition, encouraged memories, offered tea and biscuits, and cajoled visitors to nip home and bring back anything that fitted in.

But, is this writing?

The question that I kept struggling with throughout the lives of both workshops was whether this could truly be called writing? When would people pick up the pen and take off as writers? Part of this, obviously, was to do with my particular workplace experience. My role in Gatehouse was to support and encourage new writers, people who desperately wanted to write but needed to find a way round the block of their practical difficulties with writing. I would work with them to find those other routes, knowing how hard they had to struggle to work up the confidence even to begin. Getting words onto paper was a measure of their success. The next step would be to become increasingly more independent at doing that. I had to learn for myself in what way the reminiscence groups were different.

There had been lots of talking and reading in the groups. There had been pleasure at receiving typed copies of their words from the tapes. This had led onto more discussion, and different stories. Yet, the responses were always verbal. No-one went off and came back with new material that they had written. Their desire was to share memories immediately, to get a response from others straight away. So, both the needs and the aims of the reminiscence groups were on a different basis from those of other Gatehouse writing groups. They were much more interested in staying at the talking stage, having their memories teased out, remembering what they had forgotten. That was the focus, and their need was to keep the process buoyant through talk.

In the end, what took place was an exercise in group writing. Best of all, the group itself had decided that this writing was something that they wanted to make available for others to read. Both groups saw their words turned into writing and then published. They were closely involved in reviewing those words once they were written up as transcripts. The sheltered housing group piloted theirs with other groups of older people as they went out to read and talk about their memories. In turn, they listened to the words of the hospital group and used those to fire their own memories of the Blitz. In this way, the words first spoken in the group were reviewed, edited and finally approved for going public. This is the process we must all go through as writers. Their words came out in the book and the exhibition *Day In, Day Out: Memories of North Manchester from Women in Monsall Hospital*, and in the exhibition entitled 'Where Were You in the Blitz?' from the sheltered housing group. They may not have held the pen but their memories did get made permanent and that, after all, is what writing is about.

Again with both groups, there were meetings when their original tapes were read as text and worked on by them: changes were made; additions; sometimes better stories told. In this way, a definite sense of audience was created as the members moved on to make their memories public. In this instance, the reflective process that the solitary writer goes through, did start to take place.

Conclusion

Looking back at all this work, what do I now think about the implications of my expectation that these groups of older women would inevitably start to write? As a writing workshop facilitator, both the similarities and differences between groups that meet to write and those that meet to talk gradually became clear to me. In both instances, there is discussion and enjoyment of the chance to share experiences. However, in a Gatehouse writing group, invariably, by the end of the session, some of those words have been put onto paper by the group members. This means a sense of achievement, a sense of ownership and a clearer idea of what they might get from the group in future. While much of the same content is going on in the taping group, it isn't until the tape has been listened to, the dialogue written down, and then typed, that individuals can reach the same awareness of what they are so involved in. Hence the importance of that process as the spark that keeps the group running. In the meantime, however, it is the pleasure of talking and sharing that provides much more immediate feedback to the members of the group. The value of this cannot be overestimated. In my understanding, this talking meets some of the same needs that other groups achieve through writing: a sense of sharing; establishing rapport; achievement as their words are caught by others and come spinning back to weave new threads into their pictures of the past. However, in the main, it is about getting individuals comfortable enough to meet and talk together, being careful of group dynamics, providing stimulus and structure, and finding ways of making the talk available to others – providing the group agrees, obviously. I think that what works well is creating situations whereby older people have the opportunity to reminisce and to see it valued. At the same time, I do feel that it is important to do more with the group's words, to give them back to people to think about, both their originators and others.[3]

It is also important to make available in print the memories of ordinary people, not just those of the rich and powerful. In this way, it becomes possible to show the diversity of lived experience, to paint a fuller and more honest picture of history. Whether that writing comes indirectly to the page out of talking and discussion or has been the outcome of a writers' group, it matters only that it gets into print. The way we chose to work evolved in response to the particular contexts; other groups might have chosen other means or processes. Often, it is the example of what others have done that will inspire and encourage. I see this when I bring books to workshops that have been written by people similar to those in the group, whether writing about their own area or further afield. It is the fact that these lives have been considered interesting enough to publish that gets people saying, 'I could do that too!' It is important to keep people talking, and to turn that talk into writing.

Notes

1 *Write First Time* was the national literacy paper distributed regularly for ten years to literacy centres across the UK. It published writing by adult literacy students and pioneered the involvement of students as equal members of the editorial team. A comprehensive archive is lodged at the library of Ruskin College, Oxford.

2 Commonword, another North West of England community publishing group.

3 This approach to writing is supported by the Federation of Worker Writers and Community Publishers (FWWCP), a federation of writing groups which is committed to writing and publishing based on working-class experience and creativity.

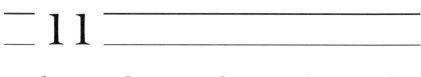

11

Arthos Wales: Working in hospitals

ROSIE MERE

The Royal Hamadryad is a psycho-geriatric hospital in the Docks area of Cardiff. In the nineteenth century, as Cardiff expanded rapidly as a port, facilities for sick seamen were expanded with the mooring in Cardiff Bay of the frigate *Hamadryad*. The ship was opened as a sixty-bed hospital in November 1866 and remained in use until a purpose-built hospital, the present Royal Hamadryad, was opened in 1905 as a general hospital. In 1972, it became a psycho-geriatric hospital and in 1975 the day hospital was opened.

All that remains today of the original hospital ship is the figurehead and the ship's bell, now on display at the nearby Industrial and Maritime Museum. The present hospital accommodates patients on three wards and the day hospital caters for an average of 25 patients from the community per day, seven days a week. It was at the Royal Hamadryad that Arthos Wales was launched in 1989 with a series of commissioned artworks.

Entering the foyer of the Royal Hamadryad Hospital, one can see a large, beautifully executed ceramic panel by Nancy Pickard and Pat Gregory depicting the Royal Hamadryad when it was a hospital ship moored in Cardiff Bay and, on the opposite wall, following a similar theme, is a striking tapestry by Jackie Duckworth. Paintings displayed on the wards in the hospital include Wendy Lewis's 'James St Swingbridge 1940' and Ruth Thomas's 'Cardiff Memories' and 'Cardiff Yesterday'.

The reminiscence painting of James Street Swingbridge originated from a photograph taken in 1943. It is hard at first to imagine the scene, standing on the present-day site; though a number of buildings are unchanged, only a strip of grass now reveals where barges were moored. My research took me to Cardiff Library photographic collection, to talks with Bill Barrett the local historian, and the Butetown History Group, memories from the staff from the Hamadryad Hospital, and books of Cardiff's past and social history.

The painting includes various children's pastimes and games, and different forms of transport. The details are intended to spur memories of life 50 years ago, for elderly patients in the Day Hospital . . . The painting will hopefully provide a talking point for staff and patients, as well as a decorative feature for the Day Hospital.

(Wendy Lewis, Arthos artist, 1990)

Arthos Wales: a brief history

Arthos Wales (Arts in Hospital Trust) was established as a charitable trust in 1988 to improve the healing environment – in hospitals, residential homes, clinics and other similar settings in South Wales – through the use of creative arts. The organization was launched in Wales in 1989 with the series of commissioned artworks described above, for the Royal Hamadryad Hospital.

In those early days, it was an entirely visual arts organization, with a small core of artists working to commission, and maintaining a loose organizational structure – enough to attract initial funding and to deal with basic administrative tasks. Overall responsibility for the organization lay with the trustees of the original Arthos based in Bristol, which now supported Arthos Wales legally but recognized it as an independent and autonomous organization. In 1989, conditions existed which set the scene for changes which were to alter the face of Arthos Wales and herald in a new and greatly extended programme of work.

While reasonable funding had been found through local government and some small charitable trusts to establish the new organization and fund several projects, this funding was obviously not going to last for ever and would have to be constantly renewed. More energy would be required to making funding applications. Securing funding for visual arts only meant that sources were more limited than for an organization with a wider working brief, while limitations of funds and the maintenance of an administrative infrastructure meant that energies were diverted from artistic endeavours to try and keep the organization solvent and efficiently run.

The active members, few in number, were first and foremost artists, and administrative tasks competed for time required to produce art works. Expansion of the programme, and therefore membership, would enable Arthos Wales to extend the range of skills within the group, releasing creative energies from the mundane administrative tasks which could be more widely shared without a great deal more financial cost.

It was also crucial to extend the range of creative arts programmes which Arthos Wales could offer client groups. As a purely visual arts organization, funding had very limited parameters and was available through limited sources. To extend the programme would also open up new sources of funding and make the organization much more broadly based in terms of both expertise and the attraction of funds.

It had also become increasingly obvious to some Arthos members through discussions with hospital staff and management, that there was considerable room, as well as expressed need, for expansion in quality hospital arts provision in South Wales. This expansion would also allow for the development of resources, expertise and work practices within a context which addressed the needs and conditions existing in Wales. For example, individual artists working with Arthos Wales who were experienced in facilitating reminiscence work, were concerned at the poor reminiscence practice they had observed within some hospitals and residential homes, often reflecting and consolidating ageist attitudes found within the institution generally and in the wider society. Also, attitudes towards the use of reminiscence were often limited to perceiving it as just another activity, the major benefit of which was to fill part of often extremely long and boring days for residents.

The most easily available resources were generally produced in England, seen as very expensive and therefore beyond the budgets of most groups, and reflected a specifically English lifestyle and history; most training opportunities of a high standard could only be found in other parts of Britain, and most practice in institutional settings, although generally provided with the best of intentions, seemed somewhat *ad hoc* both in provision and practice. Developing good practice within reminiscence work was to become a major part of the new Arthos Wales.

Changes

The first stage in the development of the new Arthos Wales was to establish a set of guidelines which would reflect the style of work practice most conducive to Arthos Wales artists as well as offer most benefit to the client hospitals. They would also reflect philosophical beliefs of Arthos Wales members in the empowerment of individuals no matter what their social status, health, status within an institution – whether as a patient, member of staff or member of management – or previous involvement in the creative arts.

The guidelines were developed partly in response to the feedback received from hospital staff and management in regard to existing programmes, and partly in consideration of the experience and skills of artists as they had developed over many years of collective experience in teaching, arts provision, training and work within institutionalized care settings in hospitals, residential homes and prisons. The guidelines focused on four main areas: quality of service; consultation and joint development of programmes between Arthos Wales, hospital staff and management and patients; staff training as an integral feature of all Arthos programmes; and recognition of the need to develop practice which reflected the culture and life of Wales. These remain the cornerstone of the work of Arthos Wales and are relatively unchanged, albeit more finely tuned, since they were developed at the end of 1989.

Quality of work in planning, content and presentation, is paramount with programmes being tailor-made to suit the needs of particular client groups. To ensure this happening, close consultation is required at all stages of a programme, including consultation with patients and staff through ongoing evaluation, both written and verbal. The ownership of programmes is taken by the hospital and those directly involved in activities – staff and patients – and this is most likely to occur if each programme is developed by all concerned as a joint venture. Process is, in this context, just as important as content.

Staff training within Arthos Wales programmes is considered to be vital for the development of good work practice and, at the initial stages of planning, departments within which activities take place are encouraged to invite the most senior staff available to be involved as participants/observers on a regular basis. The close involvement of senior staff is extremely important to the success of a programme and the wisdom of this has been borne out time and time again. Senior staff gain an in-depth understanding of the processes which are taking place within a group and the outcomes of such processes. Feedback received from staff also suggests that junior members of staff or students on placement who participate, are more likely to take the work being done seriously if senior staff are seen to be closely involved and interested in the project.

Finally, hospital management is more likely to view a programme as a valuable and cost-effective activity if favourable outcomes are relayed to it from highly qualified and knowledgeable staff who have been closely involved at all stages. The nucleus of senior and other staff attending each group session learn through observation and participation and take an active role in decision-making, offering a direct input of ideas and procedures and evaluating the programme on a weekly as well as overall basis. As wide a range of professional staff as possible is encouraged to participate and a single programme may involve occupational therapy, management, nursing and auxiliary staff, as well as students on placement.

While staff training is such a feature of Arthos work, overall quality of service and consultation are considered to be equally important. Close consultation results in a high level of trust being established between all involved from the beginning of a programme. Maintenance of this trust is crucial to the efficient use of time and resources as well as maintaining good working relationships. Similarly, overall high quality of service engenders trust and confidence in the provider, allowing the work to continue without serious delays or misunder-standings, and also builds a solid foundation for future projects.

In reflecting the culture and life of Wales, the area that had to be most urgently addressed was the gathering and developing of resource materials which were of relevance to people in Wales. Within the reminiscence programmes, for example, photograph packs of London landmarks or rural life in England, while interesting in themselves and often well-produced, did not reflect the daily lives and history of Wales and of those living in Wales. It was important to recognize that Wales had a strong and vibrant culture of its own and its people deserved to hear their own authentic voice speaking. Such resources were not easy to come by and many had to be developed group by group, with group members, hospital staff and Arthos staff providing materials from their own private sources. Since this time, more and more professionally produced resources have become available through such facilities as the excellent library established by the Service Development Team at the Royal Hamadryad Hospital. Practice also, needed to reflect the cultural realities of Wales. Arthos Wales was fortunate in having fluent Welsh speakers within the team as well as a diversity of other interests in Welsh culture and community which were able to be utilized in developing programmes.

The Arthos programmes

Programmes in reminiscence and creative writing were established at Sully Hospital, with day patients from Morfa Day Hospital with moderate to severe memory loss, and with patients receiving psychiatric care in Gwynedd Ward.

After the initial eleven-week programme was concluded, these groups became the responsibility of patients and staff. The creative writing group was continuing as strongly as ever two and a half years later. Further requests for reminiscence and life-story programmes were made by both staff and patients.

At the Royal Hamadryad Hospital, a reminiscence group was established which was to prove to be a great success:

> I would like to stress how much the patients gained from these sessions, often stating how they enjoyed them. The groups became an integral part of the occupational therapy programme and are now missed very much.
>   (Andrea Prance, Senior Occupational Therapist, 1991)

For the staff at the hospital, as well as for Arthos Wales, the Royal Hamadryad art and reminiscence activities were to be a great success, developing a far more varied programme and continuing far beyond the time-scales established originally. Equally successful were the multi-disciplinary programmes in reminiscence/art and life-story/creative writing as established at the University Hospital of Wales, Cardiff, the senior teaching hospital in the country. Soon the Arthos repertoire was extended to include dance. Memories, creative skills and creative expression intertwined to provide a rich mix of new experience, increased communication, skill development and just plain fun.

Two years later, the new-look Arthos Wales was well-established and building on a rapidly growing reputation for providing high-quality, innovative and exciting arts programmes for staff and patients in several major hospitals while also developing staff training.

A life-story focus for Arthos

Life-story work, first presented at the University Hospital of Wales, was particularly exciting and innovative and provided the model for much subsequent reminiscence work by Arthos.

Occupational therapy staff in the Department of Psychiatric Medicine at the hospital made a request to Arthos Wales for a group-based activity for a number of older women suffering from various forms of depression. Several of the women had been in contact with the hospital for many years, either as in-patients or day patients, while others had become involved in treatment more recently. Some were suffering the effects of institutionalization or the side-effects of long-term drug use, and others profound trauma and loss.

If there was one common element they all shared, however, it was a serious loss of self-esteem coupled with a sense of a life devalued as a result of their depression. All of them were very aware of being 'ill' and different and had experienced to some extent ongoing loss as a consequence of this difference – family, jobs, money, status and, most particularly, a sense of self-worth.

As the person organizing the reminiscence activities of Arthos Wales, as well as running this particular programme, I found it a challenge to find the format and style this particular group could take. The fairly traditional model, used frequently in institutional settings and based on set themes each week, such as childhood, celebrations, work, family and so on, seemed to be inappropriate here, designed as it was mainly for working with older people and in entirely different circumstances. But, as yet we had no other model to use. The question was how best to create a group which would give the individuals within it maximum opportunity for creativity and self-expression, in a setting which was safe and also challenging.

The group evolved after several lengthy discussions between myself and hospital staff as to the form it would take and who would participate. There were no unrealistic expectations either on my part or from hospital staff, as to how successful the outcomes might be. In the circumstances, some commitment to being there each week would, in itself, be an indicator of success. I began the group in traditional style keeping the discussion on very broad topics such as games and holidays, but it became apparent within three weeks that not a great deal was happening and this style was, as often as not, leaving some people feeling drained rather than stimulated or interested. In consultation with an occupational therapy student, Jacqui Rowan, who had worked with me on the group from the beginning, as well as other departmental staff, I decided to introduce elements of work I had begun to research and develop some years earlier in Sydney, using metaphor for the telling of one's life-story (Mere 1992).

The main hypothesis of this work is that when we are highly stressed and attempting to describe events and experiences which are extremely confusing, dense or complex, metaphor can provide a way into understanding. Developing metaphors which break our big, difficult story down into a series of small, colourful and often entertaining 'stories', can enable us, with a certain measure of safety and confidence, to start listening to ourselves again, and to share ourselves with others. Certainly with this group, changes in response from the first three weeks to those that followed, were remarkable. Humour became more apparent and a lightness of approach by participants began to develop as individuals began to play with their stories and creatively reconstruct them.

Asking someone 'when did you first realize you were grown up?' proved to be much more effective at providing a way into a memory than asking directly about a major life-event such as marriage or courtship where there might have been lack of a framework in which to discuss such topics. Re-evaluation of experience was also much more apparent than in more traditional groups. When given the right to decide at which level to approach a subject, the participant was much more relaxed and also took more interest in the process itself. An example of this concerns the tape-recording of sessions.

A decision had been taken not to record the sessions as it may have been considered threatening and intrusive for participants, so it was quite a surprise when, in week five, one participant voluntarily requested the sessions to be recorded for future reference – a request supported by all the other members of the group. A good lesson to be learnt here is not to make decisions without proper consultation, in this case with the participants. We had let ourselves down by not attending to our own guidelines properly. The response of the participants and staff to the programme was extremely positive, with both expressing their enjoyment of the experience and requesting further similar programmes.

Staff, in consideration of the total programme of Arthos Wales work, including the Life-Story programme as well as the creative writing and painting and drawing groups, provided some very positive feedback:

The groups have proved invaluable in so many ways:
1 Motivating staff in unit.
2 Motivating patients:
    (a) to attend regularly and to take on a commitment;
    (b) to explore their problems in a different medium;
    (c) to interact with other patients and staff;
    (d) to allow themselves to 'enjoy' something.
3 Teaching students a new dimension, to encourage self-expression.
4 The multifaceted programme enabled people with a wide range of age and disabilities to participate.
               (Sheila Sainsbury, Senior Occupational Therapist, 1991)

The Life-Story group was, however, very special, and confirmed for me the profoundly positive effect such an experience can have on individuals. The telling of the life lived, done in creative ways, can be a pathway to growth in helping build self-confidence, regain self-esteem and extend self-knowledge. It can also provide an important path for moving toward others.

While most of the reminiscence groups which Arthos Wales has offered since this time have been more traditional in style, the learning which came from this particular group has been significant in developing work practice which pays a great deal of attention to process and group building and the art of storytelling.

Reminiscence as storytelling

The reminiscence work of Arthos is closer to the life-story approach with its emphasis on empowerment of the individual and the experience of storytelling, rather than the oral history method with an emphasis on the collection of stories. This is not to negate oral history methods, but simply to understand that the life-story approach lies closer to the art of the storyteller rather than the art of the historian.

Within the life-story process, the storyteller sets the agenda and is in the position of power regarding what is to be told and how. The role of the group leader or the reminiscence worker in a one-to-one session, is that of facilitator:

The role of the worker is to help the storyteller remember and relate those stories that are of personal importance, and share them with others.
               (Beryl Ruben, Reminiscence Worker, 1990)

The programmes of Arthos Wales attempt to build on the expertise of individuals as storytellers, in visual, written, verbal and performance formats and to engage participants in recognizing their own story as an act of creativity and finding ways in which to express and celebrate it.

Within each individual, the potential for creativity is enormous and expression of this creativity adds immeasurably to quality of life. It is not difficult, therefore, to imagine how – particularly for those who for various reasons are confined to hospitals or residential homes on a long-term basis, or visit regularly as out-patients or day patients – opportunities to participate in the creative arts can be extremely important. Unfortunately, such access in most hospitals and homes is limited, if it exists at all.

Barbara Myerhoff (1978), the American anthropologist and pioneer of reminiscence practice, calls us *Homo narrens*: humankind the storyteller. The telling of stories answers a deep human need – what Beryl Ruben, in reminiscence group working notes, calls 'the need to say "I am here".' The forms this expression may take are many and various from the reminiscence narrative of 'I remember when', or through the poem:

> I am walking in the place where I was born
> The trains no longer run
> The mine is closed.
> No-one walks along the paths we walked
> . . . No smoke rises from the chimneys.
>
> (Member of UHW creative writing group, 1991)

What Rzetelny (1988) calls the 'telling of lives' forms a tradition of plenty, from the telling of the Dreamtime to the sophisticated video diaries of late twentieth-century technology.

Reminiscence is not just for older people and neither is it just about the past. It is a dynamic process in which there is a seamless quality where past, present and future ebb and flow, backwards and forwards. The importance of the act of reminiscence lies not in feats of memory but in the speaking of one's own life and having that voice listened to with an awareness of its unique qualities.

In the tape-recordings made of reminiscence sessions at the Royal Hamadryad Hospital, one will find few narratives with a beginning, middle and end. However, there are wonderful stories which have a beautiful poetic and haunting quality about them:

> I used to love going to James Howells, where the shop walker, a very smart man in a black and pin stripe suit used to come and say: 'Can I help you, Madam?', and he'd bring the chair, a nice high-backed chair, and I'd get myself on the chair, 'And one for the lady?', he'd say to me. And then he'd say: 'Now, how can I help you, what would you like?'
>
> 'Well, I want some material for a costume . . .', they didn't call them suits in those days, it was a costume, and he'd say 'think I remember your favourite colour, Madam', and she'd say, 'Do you?'
>
> 'Bottle green?'
>
> And she'd have a suit made – she liked bottle green – nothing loud you know. But he'd remember, and he'd bring down great bolts of cloth to her and fashion it all out, and my cousin, she was a lovely dressmaker, and she'd make lovely suits. She made all our clothes, actually.
>
> (Member of a Royal Hamadryad reminiscence group, 1991)

And one collective story will yield not only a treasure trove of information, but will also weave a story of pure magic from one simple question:

> R: Do you remember the gypsies?
> D: Yes, they used to go on the very rough land and they were very rough too. They'd come about once a year and have various things that they had brought along.

[Another voice . . . 'ribbons']
D: Yes, ribbons.
St: Didn't they used to sell dried flowers?
[Other voices . . . 'and mend pots . . . and umbrellas . . . sharpen knives. . .']
J: Do you remember the horses and the beautifully painted carriages?
D: I think they had tents, didn't they?
St: They didn't live in the beautiful caravans like they do today.
D: No, but when they did, they had lovely caravans.
J: Round, semi-round – pull in at the bottom and sit in the front behind the horses.
St: They're still there today, on the lay-by.
J: Do you remember the one thing you had to do – come on? My mother always used to say to me 'Who's that?', and I'd say 'It's the gypsies. . .'.
St: And she'd say 'Cross their palms with silver'.
J: And she'd say 'Here take this', and she'd put a couple of bob in their hand, and they'd say, 'Thank you very much, Madam', and away they'd go. But, if you didn't, my mother used to say, 'I wonder if it's true what they say?'
R: What was supposed to happen if you didn't?
J: Oh, they'd threaten you with all sorts of things.
St: They'd put a curse on you. They'd never say what the curse was but they used to get quite . . . if you didn't buy anything.
J: That's right. They used to say . . .
St: A curse on this house . . . something terrible like that!
J: They used to say 'Look at Mrs Morgan. You saw what happened to Mr Morgan, well, you don't want that, do you?' Isn't that right?

(Members of Sully reminiscence group, 1991)

Conclusion

There is an important place for creativity and creative expression in the lives of us all. Reminiscence is one such form of creativity, and institutions such as those in which Arthos Wales works, is one setting where these may take place.

There is a very important place, however, in such institutions for the creative arts to flourish as an expression of humanity and not only as a 'therapeutic' device. The creative arts have an important role to play in the healing process and deserve to be seen as a basic human right perhaps above and beyond all other considerations.

Finally, it is most important that the highest possible standards of work be established and maintained with safeguards, such as those developed by Arthos Wales through constant consultation, monitoring and feedback, a feature of all practice.

There is still a great deal to be done in establishing good practice, in developing a considered and widely accepted code of ethical practice, and in staff training in homes, hospitals, colleges and other institutions, and it can be done. Reminiscence can be a very magical place, and keeping the magic alive requires discipline, good practice, intelligence and sensitivity. As Gibson (1991) says, 'reminiscence deserves our very best efforts'.

References

Abbs, P. (1983) Autobiography: quest for identity. In Ford, B. (ed.), *The New Pelican Guide to English Literature. 8. The Present*, pp. 509–522. Harmondsworth: Penguin.

Adams, J. (1984) Reminiscence in the geriatric ward: An undervalued resource. *Oral History*, (12)2: 54–9.

Adams, J. (1986) Anamnesis in dementia: Restoring a personal history. *Geriatric Nursing*, September/October, 6(5): 25–7.

Adams, J. (1987) I remember, I remember. *Geriatric Nursing and Home Care*, 7(1): 9–11.

Arber, S. and Ginn, J. (1991) *Gender and Later Life: A Sociological Analysis of Resources and Constraints*. London: Sage.

Arendt, H. (1958) *The Human Condition*. Chicago, IL: University of Chicago Press.

Atkinson, D. (1991) *Past Times*. Unpublished.

Atkinson, D. and Williams, F. (eds) (1990) *'Know Me as I Am': An Anthology of Prose, Poetry and Art by People with Learning Difficulties*. London: Hodder and Stoughton.

Baines, S., Saxby, P. and Ehlert, K. (1987) Reality orientation and reminiscence therapy: A controlled cross-over study of elderly confused people. *British Journal of Psychiatry*, 151: 222–31.

Baldwin, N., Harris, J., Littlechild, R. and Pearson, M. (1993) *Residents' Rights: Key Issues in the Power to Care for Older People*. Aldershot: Avebury.

Barrowclough, C. and Flemming, I. (1986) *Goal Planning with Elderly People*. Manchester: Manchester University Press.

Bazant, J. (1992) *Personal Recollections and Music: A Review*. Leicester: Psychology Department, University of Leicester.

Becker, H. S. (1964) Personal change in adult life. *Sociometry*, 27: 40–53.

Bender, M. (1991a) The social and clinical uses of reminiscence with persons who have long term disadvantage. Paper presented at *Reminiscence Reviewed*, the Annual Conference of the Oral History Society, Lancashire Polytechnic, Preston, Lancashire, March.

Bender, M. P. (1991b) What can an applied psychologist usefully tell a librarian about oral history and reminiscence work? *Reading Therapy Newsletter* 3(1): 5–10.

Bender, M. P. (1992) Reminiscence in a museum. *Reading Therapy Newsletter*, 4: 9–16.

Bender, M. P. and McKiernan, F. (1990) The effects of reminiscence groups for elderly persons with severe dementia. Paper presented to the *London Conference of the British Psychological Society*, City University, December.

Bender, M. P., Norris, A. and Bauckham, P. (1987) *Groupwork with the Elderly*. London: Winslow.

Bender, M. P., Lloyd, C. and Cooper, A. (1990) *The Quality of Dying*. Bicester: Winslow Press.

Bender, M. P. and Tombs, D. *et al.* (1992) How should we measure the effects of groupwork with adults with learning difficulties? Part One, *Clinical Psychology Forum*, May, pp. 2–6; Part Two, *Clinical Psychology Forum*, June, pp. 3–5.

Biggs, S. (1990) Ageism and confronting ageing: Experiential groupwork to examine attitudes to older age. *Practice*, 4(2): 50–65.

Billig, M. (1987) *Arguing and Thinking: A Rhetorical Approach to Social Psychology*. Cambridge: Cambridge University Press.

Billig, M. (1989) Collective memory, ideology and the British Royal Family. In Middleton, D. and Edwards, D. (eds), *Collective Remembering*. London: Sage.

Billig, M., Condor, S., Edwards, D. *et al.* (1988) *Ideological Dilemmas: A Social Psychology of Everyday Thinking*. London: Sage.

Birren, J. E. and Deutchman, D. E. (1991) *Guiding Autobiography Groups for Older Adults*. London: Johns Hopkins University Press.

Bloch, S. and Crouch, E. (1985) *Therapeutic Factors in Group Psychotherapy*. Oxford: Oxford University Press.

Boden, D. and Bielby, D. (1983) The past as resource: A conversational analysis of elderly talk. *Human Development*, 26: 208–319.

Boden, D. and Bielby, D. (1986) The way it was: Topical organization in elderly conversation. *Language and Communication*, 6: 73–89.

Bornat, J. (1985) Reminiscence: The state of the art. *New Age*, Summer, pp. 14–15.

Bornat, J. (1989) Oral history as a social movement: Reminiscence and older people. *Oral History*, 17(2): 16–24.

Bornat, J. (1992) The communities of community publishing. *Oral History*, 20(2): 23–31.

Bornat, J. (1993) Representations of community. In Bornat, J., Pereira, C., Pilgrim, D. and Williams, F. (eds), *Community Care: A Reader*. London: Macmillan.

Bornat, J. and Adams, J. (1992) Models of biography and reminiscence in the nursing care of frail elderly people. In Via, J. M. and Portella, E. (eds), *Proceedings of the 4th International Conference on Systems Science in Health–Social Services for the Elderly and Disabled*, Vol. II, pp. 1016–28. Barcelona: A. Camps.

Boulton, J., Gully, V., Matthews, L. and Gearing, B. (1987) Developing the biographical approach in practice with older people. Project Paper 7 of *Care for Elderly People at Home*, a research and development project in collaboration with Gloucester Health Authority. Milton Keynes: The Open University, Department of Health and Social Welfare.

Bowl, R. (1981) Critical perspectives on social work with older people. In Glendenning, F. (ed.), *Social Work with Older People: New Perspectives*. Keele: Beth Johnson Foundation/University of Keele.

Brink, T. L. (1979) *Geriatric Psychotherapy*. New York: Human Sciences Press.

Bromley, D. B. (1988) *Human Ageing: An Introduction to Gerontology*. Harmondsworth: Penguin.

Bromley, D. B. (1990) *Behavioural Gerontology: Central Issues in the Psychology of Ageing*. Chichester: John Wiley.

Bruner, J. S. (1991) Self-making and world-making. *Journal of Aesthetic Education*, Summer, 25(1): 65–78.

Buchanan, K. and Middleton, D. J. (1993) Discursively formulating the significance of reminiscence in later life. In Coupland, N. and Nussbaum, J. (eds), *Discourse and Lifespan Development*. Newbury Park, CA: Sage.

Burnham, J. B. (1986) *Family Therapy*. London: Routledge.

Burnside, I. and Haight, B. K. (1992) Reminiscence and life review: Analysing each concept. *Journal of Advanced Nursing*, 17: 855–62.

Bury, M. and Holme, A. (1990) Positive images and the oldest old. Paper presented at the *Annual Conference of the British Society of Gerontology*, Durham, September.

Butler, R. N. (1963) The life review: An interpretation of reminiscence in the aged. *Psychiatry*, 26: 65–76.

Butler, R. N. (1975) *Why Survive?* New York: Harper and Row.

Bytheway, B. and Johnson, J. (1990) On defining ageism. *Critical Social Policy*, 23: 127–39.

Carter, J. (1981–82) Long ago but not (quite) forgotten. *New Age*, Winter, pp. 28–30.

CCETSW (1991) *Rules and Requirements for the Diploma in Social Work*. London: CCETSW.

CCETSW (1992) *Quality Work with Older People*. Improving Social Work Education and Training 12. London: CCETSW.

Chubon, S. (1980) A novel approach to the process of life review. *Journal of Gerontological Nursing*, 10: 543–6.

Cohler, B. J. (1982) Personal narrative and the life course. In Baltes, P. B. and Brim, O. G. Jr (eds), *Life-span Development and Behavior*, Vol. 4, pp. 205–241. New York: Academic Press.

Cole, T. R., Van Tassel, D. D. and Kastenbaum, R. (eds) (1992) *Handbook of the Humanities and Aging*. New York: Springer.

Coleman, P. G. (1974) Measuring reminiscence characteristics from conversation as adaptive features of old age. *International Journal of Aging and Human Development*, 5: 281–94.

Coleman, P. G. (1986) *Ageing and Reminiscence Processes: Social and Clinical Implications*. Chichester: John Wiley.

Coleman, P. G. (1991) Ageing and life history: The meaning of reminiscence in later life. In Dex, S. (ed.), *Life and Work History Analyses: Qualitative and Quantitative Developments*. London: Routledge.

Cornwell, J. (1984) *Hard-earned Lives: Accounts of Health and Illness from East London*. London: Tavistock.

Cornwell, J. and Gearing, B. (1989) Biographical interviews with older people. *Oral History*, 17(1): 36–43.

Corrigan, P. and Leonard, P. (1978) *Social Work Practice Under Capitalism: A Marxist Approach*. Basingstoke: Macmillan.

Coupland, J., Coupland, N., Giles, H. and Henwood, K. (1991) Formulating age: Dimensions of age identity in elderly talk. *Discourse Processes*, 14(1): 87–106.

Cowgill, D. O. (1984) The disengagement of an aging activist: The making and unmaking of a gerontologist. In Spicker, S. F. and Ingman, S. R. (eds), *Vitalizing Long-term Care*, pp. 221–8. New York: Springer.

Crawford, K., Kippax, S. and Onyx, J. (1992) *Emotion and Gender: Constructing Meaning from Memory*. London: Sage.

Cumming, E. and Henry, W. (1961) *Growing Old: The Process of Disengagement*. New York: Basic Books.

Dant, T., Carley, M., Gearing, B. and Johnson, M. (1990) *Final Report of Care for Elderly People at Home*, a research and development project in collaboration with Gloucester Health Authority. Milton Keynes: Open University.

Department of Health and Social Security (1979) Reminiscence aids: The use of audio-visual presentations to stimulate memories in old people with mental infirmity. Unpublished report.

di Gregorio, S. (1986) Understanding the 'management' of everyday living. In Phillipson, C., Bernard, M. and Strang, P. (eds), *Dependency and Interdependency in Old Age: Theoretical Perspectives and Policy Alternatives*. London: Croom Helm.

di Gregorio, S. (1987) 'Managing' – a concept for contextualising how people live their later lives. In di Gregorio, S. (ed.), *Social Gerontology: New Directions*. London: Croom Helm.

Disch, R. (ed.) (1988) *Twenty Five Years of the Life Review: Theoretical and Practical Considerations*. New York: Haworth Press.

Dobrof, R. (1984) Introduction: A time for reclaiming the past. In Kaminsky, M. (ed.), *The Uses of Reminiscence: New Ways of Working with Older Adults*. New York: Haworth Press.

Docker Drysdale, B. (1968) *Therapy in Child Care: Collected Papers*. Harlow: Longmans.

Docker Drysdale, B. (1973) *Consultation in Child Care: Collected Papers*. Harlow: Longmans.

Duffin, P. (1992) *Then and Now: A Training Pack for Reminiscence Work*. Manchester: Gatehouse Books.

Edinberg, M. A. (1985) *Mental Health Practice with the Elderly*. Englewood Cliffs, NJ: Prentice-Hall.

Elder, G. (1977) *The Alienated: Growing Old Today*. London: Readers and Writers Publishing Cooperative.

Eleftheriades, S. (1991) Remember, remember. . . . *Social Work Today*, 25 April, p. 26.

Erikson, E. (1950) *Childhood and Society*. New York: Norton.

Estes, C. (1979) *The Aging Enterprise*. San Francisco, CA: Jossey-Bass.

Evers, H. (1981) Care or custody? The experience of women patients in long-stay geriatric wards. In Hutter, B. and Williams, G. (eds), *Controlling Women: The Normal and the Deviant*, pp. 108–130. London: Croom Helm.

Feil, N. (1982) *Validation: The Feil Method. How to Help Disoriented Old–Old*. Cleveland: Edward Feil Publications.

Feil, N. (1992) Validation therapy with late-onset dementia populations. In Jones, G. M. M. and Miesen, B. M. L. (eds), *Care-giving in Dementia: Research and Implications*, pp. 199–217. London: Tavistock.

Fido, R. and Potts, M. (1989) It's not true what was written down: Experiences of life in a mental handicap institution. *Oral History*, 17(2): 31–4.

Fielden, M. A. (1990) Reminiscence as a therapeutic intervention with sheltered housing residents: A comparative study. *British Journal of Social Work*, 20(1): 21–44.

Ford, J. and Sinclair, R. (1987) *Sixty Years On: Women Talk About Old Age*. London: The Women's Press.

Frankl, V. E. (1973) *Psychotherapy and Existentialism: Selected Papers on Logotherapy*. Harmondsworth: Penguin.

Froggatt, A. (1988) Self-awareness in early dementia. In Gearing, B., Johnson, M. and Heller, T. (eds), *Mental Health Problems in Old Age*. Chichester: John Wiley.

Froggatt, A. (1990) *Family Work with Elderly People*. Basingstoke: Macmillan.

Fry, P. S. (1983) Structured and unstructured reminiscence training and depression among the elderly. *Clinical Gerontologist*, 1: 15–37.

Gatehouse (1985) *Day In, Day Out: Memories of North Manchester from Women in Monsall Hospital*. Manchester: Gatehouse Books.

Gearing, B. and Dant, T. (1990) Doing biographical research. In Peace, S. M. (ed.), *Researching Social Gerontology: Concepts, Methods and Issues*, pp. 143–59. London: Sage.

Gibson, F. (1984) *Do You Mind the Time? Northern Ireland Recall*. London: Help the Aged.

Gibson, F. (1987) *An Evaluative Study of Group Reminiscence Work*. Belfast: DHSS(NI).

Gibson, F. (1989a) *Using Reminiscence: A Training Pack*. London: Help the Aged.

Gibson, F. (1989b) *Reminiscence with Individuals and Groups: A Training Manual*. London: Help the Aged.

Gibson, F. (1991) Ordinary and extraordinary. *Reminiscence*, June.

Goldfarb, A. I. and Turner, H. (1953) Psychotherapy of aged persons. *American Journal of Psychiatry*, 109: 916–21.

Greene, R. R. (1982) Life review: A technique for clarifying roles in adulthood. *Clinical Gerontologist*, 1: 59–67.

Grele, R. (1991) *Envelopes of Sound: The Art of Oral History*, 2nd ed. New York: Praeger.

Gutmann, D. L. (1980) Psychoanalysis and aging: A developmental view. In

Greenspan, S. I. and Pollock, G. H. (eds), *The Course of Life: Psychoanalytic Contributions Towards Understanding Personality Development. Vol. III: Adulthood and the Aging Process*, pp. 489–517. Washington, DC: US Department of Health and Human Services.

Gutmann, D. L. (1987) *Reclaimed Powers: Towards a New Psychology of Men and Women in Later Life*. New York: Basic Books.

Haight, B. K. (1988) The therapeutic role of a structured life review process in homebound elderly subjects. *Journal of Gerontology*, 43: 40–44.

Haight, B. K. (1991) Reminiscing: The state of the art as a basis for practice. *International Journal of Aging and Human Development*, 33(1): 1–32.

Haight, B. K. (1992) The structured life-review process: A community approach to the ageing client. In Jones, G. M. M. and Miesen, B. M. L. (eds), *Care-giving in Dementia: Research and Implications*, pp. 139–61. London: Routledge.

Help the Aged Education Department (1981) *Recall Users' Handbook*. London: Help the Aged.

Hemmings, S. (1983) *A Wealth of Experience: The Lives of Older Women*. London: Pandora.

Hildebrand, P. (1986) Dynamic psychotherapy with the elderly. In Hanley I. and Gilhooly, M. (eds), *Psychological Therapies for the Elderly*. London: Croom Helm.

Hockey, J. (1989) Residential care and the maintenance of social identity: Negotiating the transition to institutional life. In Jefferys, M. (ed.), *Growing Old in the Twentieth Century*, pp. 201–217. London: Routledge.

Hockey, J. and James, A. (1990) Metaphors of marginality: Ageing, infantilisation and personhood. Paper presented at the *Annual Conference of the British Society of Gerontology*, Durham, September.

Holden, U. and Woods, R. (1988) *Reality Orientation: Psychological Approaches to the 'Confused' Elderly*. Edinburgh: Churchill Livingstone.

Holland, C. and Rabbitt, P. (1991) Ageing memory: Use versus impairment. *British Journal of Psychology*, 82: 29–38.

Humphries, S. (1984) *The Handbook of Oral History: Recording Life Stories*. London: Inter-Action Trust.

Hurley, A. D. (1989) Individual psychotherapy with mentally retarded individuals: A review and call for research. *Research in Developmental Disabilities*, 10: 261–75.

Johnson, M. L. (1976) That was your life: A biographical approach to later life. In Munnichs, J. M. A. and van den Heuvel, W. J. A. (eds), *Dependency and Interdependency in Old Age*, pp. 147–61. The Hague: Martinus Nijhoff.

Johnson, M. L. (1978) That was your life: A biographical approach to later life. In Carver, V. and Liddiard, P. (eds), *An Ageing Population: Reader and Source Book*. London: Hodder and Stoughton.

Johnson, M. L. (1986) The meaning of old age. In Redfern S. J. (ed.), *Nursing Elderly People*. Edinburgh: Churchill Livingstone.

Johnson, M. L. (1988) Biographical influences on mental health in old age. In Gearing, B., Heller, T. and Johnson, M. L. (eds), *Mental Health Problems in Old Age*. Chichester: John Wiley.

Johnson, M. L., di Gregorio, S. and Harrison, B. (1980) *Ageing, Needs and Nutrition*. Leeds: Nuffield Centre, University of Leeds.

Johnson, M. L., Gearing, B., Carley, M. and Dant, T. (1988) *A Biographically Based Health and Social Diagnostic Technique: A Research Report*. Project Paper 4. Milton Keynes: The Open University/Policy Studies Institute.

Jones, G. M. M. and Miesen, B. M. L. (eds) (1992) *Care-giving in Dementia: Research and Implications*. London: Tavistock.

Jordan, B. (1990) *Social Work in an Unjust Society*, Brighton: Harvester Wheatsheaf.

Jorm, A. and Korten, A. (1988) A method for calculating projected increases in the number of dementia sufferers. *Australian and New Zealand Journal of Psychiatry*, 22: 183–9.

Jung, C. G. (1933) *Modern Man in Search of a Soul*. New York: Harcourt Brace Jovanovich.

Kaminsky, M. (ed.) (1984) *The Uses of Reminiscence: New Ways of Working with Older Adults*. New York: Haworth Press.

Karpf, R. J. (1982) Individual psychotherapy with the elderly. In Horton, A. M. Jr (ed.), *Mental Health Interventions for the Aging*, pp. 21–49. New York: Praeger.

Kastenbaum, R. (1987) Prevention of age-related problems. In Carstensen, L. L. and Edelstein, B. A. (eds), *Handbook of Clinical Gerontology*, pp. 322–34. New York: Pergamon Press.

Kiernat, J. M. (1984) The use of life review activity. In Burnside, I. M. (ed.), *Working with the Elderly: Group Process and Techniques*. Belmont, CA: Wadsworth.

Kimmel, D. C. (1990) *Adulthood and Aging: An Interdisciplinary Developmental View*. New York: John Wiley.

Kitwood, T. (1989) Brain, mind and dementia: With particular reference to Alzheimer's disease. *Ageing and Society*, 9: 1–15.

Kitwood, T. (1990) The dialectics of dementia: With particular reference to Alzheimer's disease. *Ageing and Society*, 10: 177–96.

Kitwood, T. (1992) Towards a theory of dementia care: Personhood and well-being. *Ageing and Society*, 12: 269–87.

Kitwood, T. and Bredin, K. (1992) Towards a theory of dementia care: Personhood and well-being. *Ageing and Society*, 12(3): 269–87.

Knight, B. (1986) *Psychotherapy with Older Adults*. Beverley Hills, CA: Sage.

Lai, A., Little, B. and Little, P. (1986) Chinatown Annie: The East End opium trade 1920–35. *Oral History*, 14(1): 18–30.

Langley, G. and Kershaw, B. (eds) (1982) Reminiscence theatre. *Theatre Papers*, 4th series. Dartington: Department of Theatre, Dartington College of Arts.

Lasch, C. (1979) *The Culture of Narcissism*. New York: Norton.

Lawrence, J. and Mace, J. (1992) *Remembering in Groups: Ideas from Reminiscence and Literacy Work*. London: Oral History Society.

Leonard, P. (1984) *Personality and Ideology: Towards a Materialist Understanding of the Individual*. Basingstoke: Macmillan.

Lesser, J., Lazarus, L. W., Frankel, R. and Havasy, S. (1981) Reminiscence group therapy with psychotic geriatric inpatients. *The Gerontologist*, 21: 291–6.

Lewis, C. (1971) Reminiscing and self-concept in old age. *Journal of Gerontology*, 26: 240–43.

Lewis, C. N. (1973) The adaptive value of reminiscence in old age. *Journal of Geriatric Psychiatry*, 6(1): 117–21.

Lewis, M. I. and Butler, R. N. (1974) Life review therapy: Putting memories to work in individual and group psychotherapy. *Geriatrics*, 29: 165–9, 172–3.

Lieberman, M. A. and Falk, J. M. (1971) The remembered past as a source of data for research on the life cycle. *Human Development*, 14: 132–41.

Lieberman, M. A. and Tobin, S. S. (1983) *The Experience of Old Age: Stress, Coping and Survival*. New York: Basic Books.

Linn, D. and Linn, M. (1974) *Healing of Memories*. New York: Paulist Press.

Lo Gerfo, M. (1980–81) Three ways of reminiscence in theory and practice. *International Journal of Aging and Human Development*, 12(1): 39–48.

Lord, K. (1992) *The Effect of Life Review on Self-esteem in Older Adults*. Report. Southampton: Department of Psychology, University of Southampton.

Lowenthal, D. (1985) *The Past is a Foreign Country*. Cambridge: Cambridge University Press.

Lowenthal, R. I. and Marrazzo, R. A. (1990) Milestoning: Evoking memories for resocialization through group reminiscence. *The Gerontologist*, 30: 269–72.

Manheimer, R. (1982) Remember to remember. In Kaminsky, M. (ed.), *All That Our Eyes Have Witnessed*. New York: Horizon Press.

Martin, J. M. (1989) Expanding reminiscence therapy. *British Journal of Occupational Therapy*, 52(11): 435–6.

Maslow, A. H. (1970) *Motivation and Personality*. New York: Harper and Row.

McAdams, D. P. (1990) *The Person: An Introduction to Personality Psychology*. San Diego, CA: Harcourt Brace Jovanovich.

McKiernan, F. and Yardley, G. (1991) Why bother? Can reminiscence groupwork be effective for elderly people with severe dementia? *PSIGE Newsletter*, June, No. 39, pp. 14–17.

McMahon, A. W. and Rhudick, P. J. (1964) Reminiscing: Adaptational significance in the aged. *Archives of General Psychiatry*, 10: 292–8.

Mere, R. (1992) Travelling on: Life-storytelling in a psychiatric day hospital. *Oral History*, 20(1): 75.

Mergler, N. L. and Goldstein, M. D. (1983) Why are there old people: Senescence as biological and cultural preparedness for the transmission of information. *Human Development*, 26: 72–90.

Merriam, S. (1980) The concept and function of reminiscence: A review of research. *The Gerontologist*, 20: 604–609.

Meyers, K. (1991) *Life Story Books*. Stirling: University of Stirling, Dementia Services Development Centre.

Middleton, D. J. and Buchanan, K. (1991) Some rhetorical resources in remembering collectively. *Multidisciplinary Newsletter for Activity Theory*, 9/10: 12–19.

Middleton, D. J. and Buchanan, K. (1993) Is reminiscence working? Accounting for the therapeutic benefits of reminiscence work with older people. *Journal of Aging Studies*, 7(3): 321–33.

Middleton, D. J. and Edwards, D. (eds) (1990) *Collective Remembering*. London: Sage.

Middleton, D. J., Buchanan, K. and Suurmond, J. (1991) Communities of memory: Issues of 're-membering' and belonging in reminiscence work with the elderly. *PSIGE Newsletter*, 40: 8–9.

Miller, E. J. and Gwynne, G. V. (1979) *A Life Apart*. London: Tavistock.

Minois, G. (1989) *History of Old Age: From Antiquity to the Renaissance*. Cambridge: Polity Press.

Molinari, V. and Reichlin, R. E. (1985) Life review reminiscence in the elderly: A review of the literature. *International Journal of Aging and Human Development*, 20: 81–92.

Moody, H. R. (1984) Reminiscence and the recovery of the public world. In Kaminsky, M. (ed.), *The Uses of Reminiscence: New Ways of Working with Older Adults*, pp. 157–166. New York: Haworth Press.

Mortimer, E. (1982) *Working with the Elderly*. London: Heinemann.

Mouratoglou, V. (1991) Older people and their families: A workshop led by Ruth Mohr and Marilyn Frankfurt of the Ackerman Institute for Family Therapy, New York. *Context*, 8: 10–13.

Mowle-Clarke, K., Brown, K. and Bender, M. (1992) Discovering the magic circle. *Therapy Weekly*, December, p. 8.

Myerhoff, B. (1978) *Number Our Days*. New York: Simon and Schuster.

Neugarten, B. L. (ed.) (1964) *Personality in Middle and Later Life*. New York: Atherton Press.

Neugarten, B. L. (1988) Personality and psychosocial patterns of aging. In Bergener, M., Ermini, M. and Stahelin, H. B. (eds.), *Crossroads in Aging*, pp. 205–218. London: Academic Press.

Neugarten, B., Havighurst, R. and Tobin, S. (1961) The measurement of satisfaction. *Journal of Gerontology*, 14: 134–43.

Norman, A. (1985) *Triple Jeopardy: Growing Old in a Second Homeland*. London: Centre for Policy on Ageing.

Norris, A. D. (1986) *Reminiscence with Elderly People*. London: Winslow Press.

Norris, A. D. (1989) Clinic or client? A psychologist's case for reminiscence. *Oral History*, 17(2): 26–30.

Norris, A. D. and Abu El Eileh, N. (1982) Reminiscing: A therapy for both elderly patients and their staff. *Nursing Times,* 78: 1368–9.

Palmore, E. B. (1971) Attitudes toward aging as shown by humor. *The Gerontologist,* 11: 181–6.

Peace, S. (1986) The forgotten female: Social policy and older women. In Phillipson, C. and Walker, A. (eds), *Ageing and Social Policy: A Critical Assessment.* Aldershot: Gower.

Phillipson, C. (1982) *Capitalism and the Construction of Old Age.* London: Macmillan.

Phillipson, C. (1989) Challenging dependency: Towards a new social work with older people. In Langan, M. and Lee, P. (eds), *Radical Social Work Today.* London: Unwin Hyman.

Potter, J. and Wetherell, M. (1987) *Discourse and Social Psychology.* London: Sage.

Potts, M. and Fido, R. (1991) *A Fit Person To Be Removed.* Plymouth: Northcote House.

Pound, E. (1956) *Sophokles. Women of Trachis: A New Version by Ezra Pound.* London: Neville Spearman.

Rabbitt, P. M. A. (1988) Social psychology, neuroscience and cognitive psychology need each other (and Gerontology needs all three of them). *The Psychologist: Bulletin of the British Psychological Society,* 12: 500–506.

Reiss, S., Levitan, G. W. and McNally, R. J. (1982) Emotionally disturbed mentally retarded people: An underserved population. *American Psychologist,* 37: 361–7.

Rowlings, C. (1981) *Social Work with Elderly People.* London: Allen and Unwin.

Rubin, D. C., Wetzler, S. E. and Nebes, R. D. (1986) Autobiographical memory across the life-span. In Rubin, D. C. (ed.), *Autobiographical Memory,* pp. 202–221. Cambridge: Cambridge University Press.

Ryan, T. and Walker, R. (1985) *Making Life Story Books.* London: British Agencies for Adoption and Fostering.

Rzetelny, H. (1988) *How to Conduct a Life Stories Project.* New York: Brookdale Centre on Aging of Hunter College.

Samuel, R. (ed.) (1975) *Village Life and Labour.* London: Routledge and Kegan Paul.

Schon, D. (1990) *The Reflective Practitioner: How Professionals Think in Action.* Aldershot: Avebury.

Schwartz, W. (1971) On the use of groups in social work practice. In Schwartz, W. and Zalba, S., *The Practice of Groupwork.* New York: Columbia.

Scrutton, S. (1989) *Counselling Older People: A Creative Response to Ageing.* London: Edward Arnold.

Shulman, L. (1979) *The Skills of Helping Individuals and Groups.* Ithaca, NY: Peacock.

Simmons, L. W. (1945) *The Role of the Aged in Primitive Society.* New Haven, CT: Yale University Press.

Sinason, V. (1992) *Mental Handicap and the Human Condition.* London: Free Association Books.

Slater, P. E. (1964) Cross-cultural views of the aged. In Kastenbaum, R. (ed.), *New Thoughts on Old Age.* New York: Springer.

Terkel, S. (1986) *Talking to Myself: A Memoir of My Times.* London: Harrap.

Thomas, G. (1990) *Afro-Caribbean Elderly People: Coping with Ageing.* Coventry: Social Care Association/University of Warwick.

Thomas, K. (1978) *Religion and the Decline of Magic.* Harmondsworth: Penguin.

Thompson, P. (1988) *The Voice of the Past: Oral History,* 2nd edn. Oxford: Oxford University Press.

Thompson, P. (1992) 'I don't feel old': Subjective ageing and the search for meaning in later life. *Ageing and Society,* 12: 23–47.

Thornton, S. and Brotchie, J. (1987) Reminiscence: A critical review of the empirical literature. *British Journal of Clinical Psychology,* 26: 93–111.

Tobin, S. S. (1989) The effects of institutionalization. In Markides, K. S. and Cooper, C. L. (eds), *Ageing, Stress and Health,* pp. 139–163. Chichester: John Wiley.

Tobin, S. S. (1991) *Personhood in Advanced Old Age.* New York: Springer.

Townsend, P. (1981) The structured dependency of the elderly: A creation of social policy in the twentieth century. *Ageing and Society*, 1: 5–28.

Verwoerdt, A. (1988) *Clinical Geropsychiatry*. Baltimore, MD: Williams and Wilkins.

Walker, A. (1981) Towards a political economy of ageing. *Ageing and Society*, 1: 73–94.

Walker, J. M., Akinsanya, J. A., Davis, B. D. and Marcer, D. (1990) The management of elderly patients with pain in the community: Study and recommendations. *Journal of Advanced Nursing*, 15: 1154–61.

Wallace, B. J. (1992) Reconsidering the life review: The social construction of talk about the past. *The Gerontologist*, 32(1): 120–25.

Wasylenki, D. A. (1989) Psychodynamics and aging. In Wasylenki, D. A., Martin, B. A., Clark, D. F., Lennox, E. A., Perry, L. A. and Harrison, M. K. (eds), *Psychogeriatrics: A Practical Handbook*. London: Jessica Kingsley.

Watt, L. M. and Wong, P. T. P. (1991) A taxonomy of reminiscence and therapeutic implications. *Journal of Gerontological Social Work*, 16(1/2): 37–57.

White, J. (1980) *Rothschild Buildings: Life in an East End Tenement Block 1887–1920*. London: Routledge and Kegan Paul.

Wong, P. T. and Watt, L. M. (1991) What types of reminiscence are associated with successful aging? *Psychology and Aging*, 6: 272–9.

Woods, B. (1992) What can be learned from studies on reality orientation? In Jones, G. M. M. and Miesen, B. M. L. (eds), *Care-giving in Dementia: Research and Implications*, pp. 139–161. London: Routledge.

Woods, B., Portnoy, S., Head, D. and Jones, G. (1992) Reminiscence and life review with older persons with dementia: Which way forward? In Jones, G. M. M. and Miesen, B. M. L. (eds), *Care-giving in Dementia: Research and Implications*, pp. 137–161. London: Routledge.

Wright, M. (1986) Priming the past. *Oral History*, 14(1): 60–65.

Yalom, I. D. (1985) *The Theory and Practice of Group Psychotherapy*. New York: Basic Books.

Index